Twice serving as an Officer in the Royal Navy, including during the first Gulf War, Manley Hopkinson's leadership skills have been developed through practice as well as study. He has at various points been an Inspector in the Royal Hong Kong Marine Police, the skipper on a 32,000 mile round-the-world yacht competition and record-setting winner of a race to the Magnetic North Pole, where his team faced polar bear attacks and sub-zero temperatures. Throughout all of this he has remained a 'leader in learning'.

As an inspirational speaker, Manley combines the two worlds of business and adventure to encourage leaders everywhere – at work, at home, in sports and mid-ocean – to take a new approach to creating teams of developed, self-aware and committed individuals. His method encourages leaders to gain commitment; rather than force compliance.

Praise for *Compassionate Leadership*:

'An excellent contribution to creating awareness on compassion' – Office of His Holiness the Dalai Lama

'A personal and most readable introduction to the fundamentals of good leadership, enlivened by the author's rich and varied experience. Anyone who aspires to be a leader will find in its pages both guidance and encouragement' – John Adair, author of the bestselling *Effective Leadership*

'We are in a time of disruptive leadership change. Compassion is our way forward. Manley has presented an abundantly wise and carefully crafted guide for all leaders to help us travel on our collective journey with ease and grace' – Sue Cheshire, founder and MD, Global Leaders Academy

'Human Beings are incredible but why is it that companies so often diminish their people's vast capability? With a clear vision, a well communicated plan and visible "compassionate leadership" in a values based culture, the power of collective brilliance enables us to achieve almost anything. This is Manley's quest; to unleash the true potential of individuals and their teams, thereby enabling their companies to consistently out perform their peer group. His approach is both disciplined and challenging, but also immensely human and the more effective for it. All that Manley advances he lives by, constantly testing and adapting. He has consistently created high performing cultures in the engagements that we have worked on together over the last seven years. This is a book well worth reading for both you and your business' – Huw Owen, Chief Executive Ark Data Centres

'I have read Manley's book *Compassionate Leadership* and found it to be a masterful business book. I say this not only because of the content and excellent approaches to business leadership and culture change but because I have lived this journey with Manley. He assisted the Teleflex International Leadership Team and the Teleflex Executive Staff in defining the values for the team, the division and ultimately the entire organisation. We travelled the journey of self-discovery using tools such as the Iceberg, aligning ourselves towards the ME YOU and US and engaging in active dialogue within our organisation. I had a good team. With the help of Manley and the tools described in this book we ended up with a GREAT team and a truly high performing organisation' – Liam Kelly, Executive Vice President and President International EMEA, APAC and India, Teleflex IDA

'When doing "business reading" I tend to annotate and dog-ear my copy of the book so I can go back to the sections which resonated most, were the most insightful or where the exercises made me stop and think. I don't think I've ever dog-eared a book as much as this! There is lots of value in that, and I'll be reading back through these highlights and weaving them into my management tool kit. *Compassionate Leadership* has plenty of pace and it was a pleasure to read, which is a rare combination.' – Guy Lister, Chief Customer and Marketing Officer, Office

'There are basically two types of worthwhile management books: those with an evidence-based foundation and those with an experience-based foundation. In the latter you want to read the thoughts and experiences of seasoned people who can convey their pearls of wisdom in an inspirational way. This is certainly the case with *Compassionate Leadership* in which you not only almost literally hear Manley speak, but you also feel as if you are travelling with him through his life and leadership experiences. And the nicest thing is that you don't have to go through all the hardship Manley encountered to profit from all his wise lessons!' – Dr André de Waal MBA, Academic director HPO Center, Associate professor Maastricht School of Management and author of *What Makes a High Performance Organization*

'Great insights based on Hopkinson's knowledge of leadership in both business and in the harsh arena of ocean sailing and Antarctic adventure. This book is backed with practical, easily remembered tools and written in an engaging style.' – Dr Andy Cave, Mountaineer, Author, Speaker

'*Compassionate Leadership* stands out in a crowded field of management and self-help literature. Manley's insights, gained from real life experience, are thoughtful and persuasive and most importantly: they work. I think the examples Manley cites apply to all relationships, not just those between manager and managed, and I recommend this book to anyone trying to lead, motivate, build or, indeed, be part of a successful team.' – Andrew Sharpe, V.P, National Conservative Convention

'*Compassionate Leadership* gives you the tools to enable each individual to bring the very best of themselves to the workplace. It's an approach ideally suited to master the leadership challenges of today and in the future.' – Paul Devoy, Head of Investors in People

Praise for Manley's speaking

'We engaged Manley to help steer us through a major change programme and the results he has delivered are exceptional. Not only does Manley have first-hand experience of major leadership challenges, but he also has the ability to communicate those experiences in a way that the team can practically engage with and use in a positive way. I would not hesitate in recommending Manley to any organisation that faces similar challenges.' – Nigel Keen, Director of Property, John Lewis Partnership

'I've worked with Manley at three separate organisations now. He brings professionalism, focus and new perspective to every assignment. His unique view on leadership and diligent research combined with his personal experience across numerous continents and exploits always brings a high-energy, engaging contribution, whether this is to a leadership programme or a conference agenda. Highly recommend.' – Simon Kettle, Head of Development and Engagement, Manchester Airport Group

'In his book and as a speaker Manley brings personal experience, academic study and humour to enable others to learn. At every turn there is insight and the opportunity to reflect on how one wishes to be as a leader, and, as fallible human beings, how we can fall short.' – Shaun Sawyer, Chief Constable, Devon and Cornwall Police

'Manley Hopkinson is the sort of man you would follow to the ends of the earth. Indeed, many have. A tall, strapping, unstoppably charismatic optimist – the sort that sees rain as "liquid sunshine" – this former naval officer has led exhibitions to the North Pole and skippered a yacht crew round the world "the wrong way", that is, into the wind, as part of the BT Global Challenge. If anyone knows about leadership, he does. Watch him and you know what leadership looks like. Listen to him and you learn what it entails.' – Ian Gray, Director, Turnaround Management Association

Manley Hopkinson

COMPASSIONATE LEADERSHIP

HOW TO CREATE AND MAINTAIN ENGAGED, COMMITTED & HIGH-PERFORMING TEAMS

piatkus

PIATKUS

First published in Great Britain in 2014 by Piatkus

7 9 10 8 6

Copyright © Manley Hopkinson 2014

A CIP catalogue record for this book
is available from the British Library.

ISBN 978-0-349-40322-9

Typeset in Aldus by M Rules
Printed and bound in Great Britain by
Clays Ltd, Elcograf S.p.A.

Papers used by Piatkus are from well-managed forests
and other responsible sources.

Piatkus
An imprint of
Little, Brown Book Group
Carmelite House
50 Victoria Embankment
London EC4Y 0DZ

An Hachette UK Company
www.hachette.co.uk

www.improvementzone.co.uk

I dedicate this book to . . . you!
Hurrah!

This book belongs to

_____

'A journey of a thousand miles begins with a single step'
– Lao Zi

'Take courage and take that step'
– Manley

CONTENTS

ACKNOWLEDGEMENTS

Many thanks go to my beautiful wife Cate, of course, for nudging me in the right direction, keeping my feet firmly on the floor and for being the mother of my two fantastic children (and an excellent one at that)! Cate, you are my inspiration in so many ways and a woman of great strength.

To my two children Frey and Arabella: I have learned so much from you about love, life and leadership. It was with you in mind that I derived the key values of awareness, courage, confidence, joy and compassion which I now apply in all walks of my life.

To my mother who, many years ago, instead of chiding me, created within me the drive and passion that has shaped my life and led to so many adventures. You are a truly inspiring person, Mum, and I love your company.

To my father, whose love of poetry and respect for his boss provided me with a great name. Although it was a tough one to own at times, particularly during my schooldays, I enjoy it very much now and have often wondered how different my life would have been not as a 'Manley'!

And to my siblings, Neil, Susan and Guy, for sharing my life, being my family, growing up with me (though some would argue I have yet to start that bit) and for their love and support.

There have been many who have helped to smooth the rough edges, fashion my thinking, join me on adventures and generally enrich my life. I thank you all; most of you were at my recent 'significant' birthday – that was fun!

To Sir Chay Blyth for his belief in the power of attitude over ability, and his support of me in his remarkable race, the BT Global Challenge – a life changer in so many ways. I also need to thank Sir Chay for his love of whisky, which fuelled the start of my 'speaking' career in New Zealand!

To the boys and girls at Mission Performance, particularly Rob Lewis and Chris McLeod, the founders and inspirers who kick started my career as it is now. We did so much together, I learned so much with you and we had so much fun along the way – thanks chaps – I am for ever indebted to you! Hurrah! Where would I be without my best chum, Whitters, with whom my pact to go to every Rugby World Cup 'until we die' has created a cadence and pattern to my life, around which all must revolve. You give me so much, my friend. Thank you.

To Huw Owen, who believed in me and gave me a step up to a new level, again and again and with whom I have learned and achieved so much.

To the Royal Navy – hurrah! – for providing me with superb grounding and early learning. The lessons on leadership, presentation skills, personal discipline, responsibility and true camaraderie have enabled me to do so much and to understand what is needed to bring a team together and what can be achieved as a result.

To Hong Kong, Papua New Guinea, South Africa, Greece, Turkey and then Italy for providing the backdrop and stage for some great adventures and a hell of a lot of learning (and more books).

To the jolly learned people like Jung and Porter, Hertzberg, Maslow and McLelland, French and Raven, Joseph Luft and Harrington Ingham and so many more that I reference in my life, my work and this book – I have learned much from you and hope that in applying your learning I have your approval!

And to John Adair, of course, to whom I am eternally grateful for your wisdom and the manner in which you shared it with the world.

Then the Professor, Andre de Waal, who read 290 books so

I did not have to, analysed them, tested them and then shared his great work on High Performance Organisation!

And finally, there were many places and people that have been witness to seminal moments in my life, but none as profound as the moment in the Trafalgar Tavern in Greenwich, London, where I made some great friends, had great fun and found my life's partner!

CHAPTER 1

WHO *IS* THIS MANLEY CHAP?

One Christmas I received a framed poster from my children saying, 'Some people wish for things to happen, some want them to happen, others make them happen.' I can relate to all three.

There's lots of stuff I wish for and much I want; but, thankfully, I do tend to *make* things happen – for me and for others. And you do rather get the point when a message is repeated by others independently and, seemingly, coincidentally.

While at an exhibition of the photographs of Leonard Huxley taken during Robert Falcon Scott's second Antarctic expedition of 1910 to 1912 (Huxley edited Scott's journals), I bumped into and was inspired by an amazing lady in her nineties, Susan Ewer. She's a daughter of the Raj, brought up in a colonial world, now bent and weathered, but with an incredible sparkle in her eye and an energy in her voice. Our worlds met as we gazed, in awe, at an iconic photograph of Scott and his men in their hut. We spoke, we connected and, in a way, we both found inspiration within each other.

Susan was moved by my desire, nay, intent, to 'go south' and pit my wits against the mightiest of continents, and I was inspired by her stories, energy and passion for life. We exchanged details and went our separate ways. It tells much for the 'discipline' and social etiquette lost over the years that, after that encounter, it was Susan who first made contact, and by letter! She wrote to say thank you and to share her thoughts. Susan felt invigorated by our meeting and shared something truly special that I have with me all the time: it's become my iPhone screensaver and my Facebook image and has fashioned much of my work since. It was a card with an inscription taken from a Sussex church *circa* 1730:

A Vision without a Task is but a Dream,
A Task without a Vision is Drudgery,
A Vision and a Task is the Hope of the World.

Within this card she wrote, in ink, in a beautiful flowing hand, 'A Dream, a Vision and a Task Accomplished is Fine Achievement and Inspiration for All.' And on the back was a quote from Franklin D. Roosevelt saying, 'The only limit to our realisation of tomorrow will be our doubts of today.'

Classic! Thank you, Susan.

That card with a 300-year-old inscription and the FDR quote from more than 200 years after that sum up, when combined, much of my attitude to life and also the concepts of what it takes to be a what I'll be calling a 'Compassionate Leader'.

My journey to the role of adviser on developing high performance in organisations, teams and individuals has not been a straightforward one. My colourful career has been as much due to my tendency to say yes to any opportunity, and to put a 'task' to that 'vision', as it has been to help others find their path and say yes, too. I have learned much along the way. Sometimes I got it right and other times very wrong. My original exploration around leadership, team and personal development was fashioned by my experiences as an adventurer, a businessman and a leadership coach, mentor and catalyst.

I was recently interviewed for a magazine and was asked, 'What makes you do these adventures? What makes you think you can do them?' Both my parents, in their own way, have created within me the thinking that I can do anything and make it work. My father, whose naval career inspired me greatly and whose natural charisma and rapport I could see impacted on those around him, clearly had, and still has, a large impact on my life as, apparently, I am becoming more and more like him every day in looks, sound and mannerisms. Cripes!

But I put it down to something my mother said when I was a small boy. I was a lively child and would frequently be pushing the boundaries and exploring what I could do. My mother was reluctant to administer corporal punishment or to physically restrain my activities – and, on this particular occasion, she was baking so it would have meant a smack round the head with a wooden spoon covered in cake mix! Instead, she said in a stern voice, 'If you do that, you must accept the consequences of your actions and redeem the situation.'

Initially, I was confused and uncertain about exactly what that meant, but it sounded serious, so it worked: I *did* stop whatever it was that I was doing and contemplated my options, just as Mum wanted. Later she was to explain what it meant: if you *do* choose to do something, then only *you* made the choice; you cannot blame someone else, so you have to accept whatever happens as a result. And, if is not a good consequence, then you need to sort it out yourself!

However, it worked in a way that my mother did not intend, although even now she congratulates herself on the 'unintended consequence' of her actions. For, as I began to understand the words within her 'threat', what I was hearing in my mind was, 'Manley, you are free to do anything, whatever you wish. There are no bounds to what you can do as long as you accept the consequences of your actions and redeem the situation!' So now, wherever I may be – be that on an ice cap, in mid-ocean or in the boardroom – I believe I *can* do anything, and I will always try, because my mother gave me the freedom to do so. And I know that I must 'accept the consequences' of my actions and 'redeem the situation'.

Funny old thing, life, as are the unintended consequences of what we say and do. Who would have thought?

*

My job as an inspector in the Royal Hong Kong Marine Police did not end up being a lifelong career. It was followed by my running and owning a boat-building and -servicing company in the Far East, and was sandwiched between twice serving as an officer in the Royal Navy. During the first stint, I attained a degree in marine engineering. The second stint, after I left Hong Kong, came when I rejoined the service for the first Gulf War. The sea is in my blood and for many years as a professional skipper I captained various craft in various oceans before coming back to Blighty to work as a marine surveyor, then applying my seaborne skills ashore as a contract project manager for Granada Media, leading one of its major Year 2000 projects. All great skills that I would apply later, on land, in the boardrooms and offices of some of the world's largest corporations.

Adventure is part of my genetic makeup. Racing around the world as a skipper in what is billed the world's toughest yacht race, the BT Global Challenge, and winning the first skiing race to the Magnetic North Pole in record time have provided excellent training for other adventures, great stories to tell and a lot of learning along the way.

I am working on other 'expeditions' as I write. As an adviser and mentor on the topics of leadership and success, I need to be constantly testing myself and improving my understanding of what works and what doesn't. I would hate to be considered a one-trick pony!

Yet my ramblings on leadership and team working were not forged and fuelled only by quest and exploration: much has been learned in the boardrooms and on the shop floors of businesses globally. I have worked as a consultant and facilitator across so many different fields of business, and have become an integral part of many organisations within the leadership team to effect deep cultural shifts A few years back, I had the incredible opportunity to sit on the board of the ATLAS Consortium and then that of Hewlett-Packard Enterprise Services Defence & Security UK Ltd, tasked with delivering a fundamental shift in culture to enable the businesses to become what are known as high-performing organisations, or HPOs (and we'll meet this term again later). Being an accountable part of the business meant that I learned so much more by being on the inside and I could add so much more value as a result. It is a *modus operandi* I enjoy and have repeated to great effect. Today, I advise a number of corporate boards, coach senior executives and business leaders and work closely with senior leadership teams and boards effecting large-scale cultural change and delivering high business performance all over the world, each time not just sharing my stories and my learning, but growing my stories and learning too.

I learn at every corner; on the ice, at sea, in the desert and when working with leaders all over the globe – but I think I learn most from my children. I also coach kids in rugby and sailing. I believe that to be even more demanding and rewarding. Kids tend not to offer as much 'respect and attention' as adults. When they are bored or lose interest, they show it. You have to be on your toes and cannot gloss over any element of the learning. It is also a great lesson in not externalising your own motivation. Research clearly shows that kids play sport to enjoy themselves, have fun, be with mates. It is only the coaches and parents who, bellowing from the touchline, force the focus on to winning. We have so much to learn from kids! (We'll look a little more at externalising motivation later.)

My experiences have allowed me to learn at first hand about how to create and develop the transformational leadership behaviours needed for businesses, sporting teams and individuals to perform at a high level, consistently. From turning around failing teams to creating new ones, I have enabled people to gain a deeper understanding of self, and through that a better understanding of others, leading to more effective business and personal relationships.

And that is one of the fundamental premises of this book and all my experience: it comes down to understanding self first. A Compassionate Leader starts their understanding at home. Look in the mirror first: Who are you? How are you? Really? Be honest!

There is a lovely expression that says that a good leader has the smallest gap between what they do, what they say and who they are – a Compassionate Leader. I believe that simple communication facilitates understanding, and stories build memorable images. If the lesson is understood and remembered, there is a chance that behavioural changes will follow. I have inspired audiences worldwide by recounting my experiences and bringing the topics of leadership, 'team-ship' and 'self-ship' – the essences of 'relationships' – alive using powerful metaphors from my journeys to bring benefit to many of the world's leading organisations and the people within them.

My values

I was once interviewed for a magazine. The topic of discussion moved on from my adventures to my family. 'So what would you like your kids to do when they leave home?' I had to really think hard. 'I honestly don't mind what "work" they do. That's irrelevant, and, in reality, no business of mine. But, when they do fly the nest, if they have inside them some core values, then I believe that my work is best done.' That discussion afforded me the opportunity to reflect deeply on what I hold most dear, on what my biggest lessons have been and what I aspire to be. Though my answer at the time was not so succinct and clear, the subsequent deep reflection and revelation is at the heart of all I do and forms the core of Compassionate Leadership.

Having challenged, tested and refined my answer to that question, I would like to share with you my views on how we must be – the values that, if held close to our being, will guide us through the stormy and the tranquil seas to fulfil our own destiny to best effect and so help others fulfil theirs. The five values that are the foundation of Compassionate Leadership – I call them the 'Big Five' – are:

- awareness
- courage
- confidence
- joy
- compassion

I try to live by these Big Five and I try to encourage those I have an impact on to consider the same. I believe that values should not just be used to describe who you are, but should include an element of aspiration, the stretch required to become the best person you want to be and can be. I believe my role as a parent is to try to instil these values in my offspring, and my role as a leader and mentor is to help you and others understand them too. I can feel I've succeeded if, when they leave the nest, my children venture into the world with awareness, courage, confidence, joy and compassion. I feel I have been successful in any leadership development or cultural evolution programme if I can instil those core values into my audience. These do not necessarily need to be overt, visible 'corporate values' that splash the walls and inform the activity and culture in an organisation, but instead can be the culture of my interventions and a 'challenge' to the organisation's leaders to live by them as individuals, asking, 'What if?' – 'What if you tried to live by these? How would it be? How would you feel?'

Let me explain the behaviours I see that support the 'Big Five'.

Awareness

It all starts here. Nothing else can happen if we are blind to ourselves and blind to others. There is so much we need to be aware of, and I talk about that later in the book with my model 'Me, You and Us', which is about raising our 'Me Aware' and our 'You Aware' and putting them together in the 'Us Aware' space for mutual benefit (see Chapter 5). We need to know so much about what is going on within ourselves that drives our behaviour, and that very much includes being aware of our emotions. We need to understand others and, vitally, we must be aware of the impact we have on others. Being aware of 'who' we are allows us to act with that next value: courage.

Courage

I see so many people in our modern world who are detached from who they really are. The strong influences of our community and corporate world have driven us away from our core value set. We'll spend some time later exploring how that happens and what the consequences are for the individual and for society. What is set at an early age is where we want to be, but we get dragged away by external influences – schools, national cultures, churches, media, celebrity and the dominant corporate cultures. At each step we become more and more detached from who we actually are. With each new community we meet, our 'values gap' widens.

We may be aware of it or we may not – either way, it leads to internal conflict as we find that we are deprived of self-esteem. How can we relate to others when we cannot relate to ourselves? Why are so many people living other people's dreams? The courage I speak of is the courage to live your own life, your own dreams; the courage to be you within any community; the courage to take the first step on that true journey towards your own fulfilment. There is a beautiful Arabic saying: 'A journey of a thousand miles starts with a single step.' True courage is taking that step on the long journey of self.

Confidence

The confidence that I speak of is the self-belief that you can and will make it work. When others may doubt you, confidence is in not doubting yourself. Confidence allows the making of mistakes as you believe you can prevail. Confidence gives freedom.

Confidence *breeds* confidence – in yourself, in others and in your own abilities.

Sometimes, your confidence may be unfounded as you stumble and fall, but, aligned with courage, confidence sets you up to try again. Remember the old adage? 'If at first you don't succeed, try, try again.' We need confidence deep within, and we need that *awareness* we spoke of earlier to understand that, even if deep inside there are doubts (and they do exist and should not be denied), we can muster up our *courage* to act with *confidence*! I have never 'failed' at anything! Frequently, I did not get to where I wanted to be or as high as I had thought, but I learned a lesson; I was able to grow and move on. Confidence is understanding that 'not succeeding' in a specific task is not failure: it is a lesson!

Joy

I feel that so many of us have lost the 'joy of the journey'. We are caught up in a world that does not value or encourage joy; a world where it is the numbers and only the numbers that count in our unsustainable, perpetual desire for growth. Our world seems to revolve around what we can get and not what we can give, where the journey is not important and is subservient to the destination. It is not. That is wrong. The journey is where the joy is found. Feel joy in your journey, in this journey, our leadership journey. Feel and share the joy of being a leader. Enjoy life. I half-jokingly point out that we must enjoy life because the destination, death, does not sound like so much fun!

Whatever your beliefs may be for what happens or does not happen beyond this life, even if this life is the preparation for the next, then the value of joy still stands true. Create an intrinsic enjoyment of the journey. And with joy comes the feeling of 'gratitude' – being thankful feeds being joyful. As the famous saying goes, 'Smile and the whole world smiles with you'. Try it. Smile! Be joyful!

Compassion

Compassion, in essence, is having the peripheral vision to see others and help them along the journey of awareness, courage, confidence and joy. Our society has created a focus on self. We are not seeing those people around us. The Dalai Lama explains the difference between 'compassion' and 'empathy' pretty well, and I paraphrase: 'Empathy is a desire to know the other person. Compassion is to act on that knowledge with positive intent.'

As I was driving recently in my home town, an old lady was trying to cross the road but the continuous stream of traffic did not see her. I stopped to let her cross, for, after all, it would have no negative impact on my journey for such a short time. But still the traffic coming the other way did not stop. Eventually, I held out my hand to stop the oncoming traffic and beckoned towards the lady. The driver on the other side, on seeing the old lady, understood her needs and was only too happy to stop and let her cross. It is not that we did not want to help the old lady: it is that we did not 'see' her!

Compassion is about *seeing* the other, and, on seeing, then understanding and providing for their need. It is about increasing our peripheral vision, being aware of our fellows and all sentient beings on our precious planet.

Consider a dinner with a silent order of monks. How do you ask for the salt? That's the point. You don't. If the salt is in front of you and you desire it, your compassionate thinking leads you to the understanding that, if you desire something, your fellow may too, so, having salted your dinner, you naturally, without request, pass it on. On my yacht, you never made a brew for yourself. If you fancied a brew, so too, more than likely, would others in the crew. If I felt like a (very British) cup of tea, I asked all and made for all. That is a compassionate act.

I feel that if those closest to me, and within my influence, can show . . .

- *awareness* – knowing 'Me, You and Us'
- *courage* – to take that first step on their own life's journey, to be themselves
- *confidence* in themselves – that they will make it work
- *joy* in our world, the here and now, and
- *compassion* towards others

. . . then so can I; and, if I can, then so can they. It's a virtuous circle!

Above all else, this book and the whole premise of Compassionate Leadership requires the essence of these values.

This book encourages you to be more **aware** – to look deep in the mirror and to raise your awareness of your fellow person.

It aims to give you the **courage** to use it – the courage to go out there and try; the courage to take on the world or the systems you find yourself in and not just to accept mediocrity or wrong; the courage to stand up for what you know to be true; the courage to be true to yourself.

A truly profound and challenging saying attributed to Edmund Burke (and found in various versions) is, 'It is necessary only for the good man to do nothing for evil to triumph.'

So you will need **confidence** in yourself; confidence in your ability to make things happen; confidence to stand up after being knocked down; confidence that, no matter what, you can and will make it work. You will also need confidence in people around you.

As we strive for greater self-awareness in the lives we lead and the values we hold, so we will feel and share the **joy** of life. Love life. Live it to the full. Do not waste a single day – you will never get it back.

And, most importantly, even in the simplest of actions we can demonstrate **compassion**. In fact, it's in the simplest of actions that it becomes real. The everyday gesture. The smallest recognition. Be aware of those around you – of the people, the animals and the planet. Increase your peripheral vision –

see more, feel more, do more. Compassion, when we are in our true state, is an intrinsic quality of humanity.

Being a dad, a polar adventurer, a businessman, a former police inspector, a former naval officer, a yachtsman, a motivational speaker, a coach and a leadership catalyst, I have had incredible opportunities to learn about and test my ideas of leadership and teamwork. I have worked with some impressive and generous people who have given me their time and shared their wisdom; they have taught me much.

I have thoroughly enjoyed my journey so far, and my intention is to continue in the same vein. I hope *you* enjoy my adventures, too, as much as I do, and I also hope you can draw on my learning and make it part of your own. I have no doubt that by reading and applying the principles in this book, you will find that things will happen for you too.

It has been a pleasure and honour sharing it with so many. This book is for you, from me. Join me on a new journey.

And say 'Yes'!

EXERCISE: THE BIG FIVE VALUES

Let's look again at the Big Five values and how they can form an inspirational and aspirational part of one's life's journey. These were awareness, courage, confidence, joy and compassion.

The awareness ties in with the Me, You and Us model touched on earlier, but dealt with in detail in Chapter 5. How much do you know about yourself, the people you are with, the impact you make and the environment you create?

Do you have the courage to be yourself, follow your own life's journey? Do you recognise that you have your own path in life and you must dictate it? Do you have the courage also to act, move and decide?

Do you have the confidence to trust in yourself and in the people around you?   ➝

Then there's the joy of the journey. Focus on the 'how' as well as the outcome. Live in the present and enjoy the moment, develop your intrinsic motivation.

Muster the compassion not only to 'see' others to but to help them fulfil their true life's journey by being aware, courageous, confident, joyous and compassionate!

Here's what you do. Reflect on how your life and your leadership journey would be affected if you adopted these Big Five? Ask 'What if … ?'

With each value, capture its impact on you, your people and your organisation. Use the grid below.

Value	Impact on me	Impact on family, friends, team	Impact on my organisation
Awareness			
Courage			
Confidence			
Joy			
Compassion			

Notes

_____

_____

_____

_____

_____

_____

_____

_____

_____

_____

_____

_____

_____

CHAPTER 2

HOW THIS BOOK WORKS

The chapters of this book will provide you with understandable, memorable and usable ways of applying these principles and tools to your business and to your life. These are not just 'business tips': they are life-changing, life-fulfilling actions and attitudes that you can adopt and apply in all situations and relationships.

But I'm going to do something rather unusual. Before we launch into how the book works, I'm going to ask you to read Chapter 3 first. It looks at my key thinking, that is at the core of all you will learn. You'll see that I also suggest you can go from there to anywhere in the book, or you can return to here and continue reading how the book works. I'll see you back here in a while!

Right, now you're back, let me first explain the 'understandable, memorable and usable' bit, for I want you to judge my thinking and this book based on those qualities. If you can **Understand** something, then you have a chance of remembering it, of making it **Memorable**, and it is only if you can remember it that you will be able to **Use** it! You will see this referenced throughout the book as 'UMU' – Understandable, Memorable, Usable.

Understandable

I will not use jargon or management-speak. I will not use ten words when one will do. Nor will you have to wade through copious amounts of theory. I will endeavour to use plain English. I will explain my thinking and the learning and theory behind it in such a way as to make it totally accessible. I have learned much from some great thinkers who have gone before me, and, where I have used their theories, I will do so in a 'simplistic form' and encourage you to engage in further reading should you so desire, but I will be brief.

You know what? That last paragraph should have just read 'I will keep it simple.' if I was going to abide by my own rules! See? I'm learning! Every day's a school day!

Memorable

I believe in the power of stories. In Western cultures, particularly, we have forgotten their power and revert to 'telling' or 'teaching' or 'commanding' others to learn. These styles are, unsurprisingly, often rebelled against or ignored. We frequently talk about how we deal with 'teaching' kids, but adults have the same learning traits and desires. It used to be, and still is in many communities, that the wisdom of the elders was passed on from generation to generation through the telling of stories. A story evokes images, imagination and an emotional response and attachment. Stories allow people to share their knowledge and experience intertwined with the knowledge and experience of others. You can engage with a story, be a part of it, add to it and share it. It brings people together. The Aborigines talk about 'your song'. 'What's your song?' they will ask. In other words, 'Who are you? What's your story? Tell me about yourself.' I like that as a way of thinking – we all have a song inside us. I'll share my 'songs' and encourage you to find your own songs – and sing them!

I will use the power of stories throughout. I will share anecdotes from my sailing, polar travel and business life, and, through these stories, bring the theory to life. Being a modest sort of fellow, I will share stories of great success with humility, but balance them with times when things have not gone so clearly to plan. I am a firm believer that we must learn from our mistakes and we must learn through *making* mistakes. Failure is measured only in time.

Usable

So, the learning is understood and the story has provided the anchor for memory. Now we need to be able to apply it to real life, or it is all a waste of time. It is not good enough to know. It is not good enough to be motivated. You must actually *do*. It is our behaviour that counts, not our intent or understanding. It is our behaviour that others see and judge us on. Throughout this book, as I share my experiences and my learning, so I will include actions for you. There will be simple activities, tools, tips and techniques, and practical points that will be usable and constructive to you as a leader and as a human being. Each chapter is wrapped up with a reminder of the learning and clear instruction and tips on how to apply the learning. And some encouragement, too!

Old dogs, new tricks?

But it isn't just the telling of stories that will enable us to memorise these philosophies and learnings. Nor the clarity of the prose. Even the explanation of how to utilise these skills is not enough to make it stick. For that to happen, we need to develop a basic understanding of the workings of the brain. I am not a brain surgeon, but . . .

It may help us to remember, then use this book, and then help others do the same if we understand that the brain works by creating networks and associations of synaptic links. Each stimulus creates its own 'pathway' in our brains. That 'pathway' is reinforced by associated stimuli creating a network of links. Repetitive experiences consolidate these links by passing more and more electrical currents through this network of associated pathways, each time attracting fatty deposits and insulating the path, much like the insulation on an electrical wire. Soon they become 'highways' of perceptions and habits. The electrical pulses would rather travel in these highways than any weaker links nearby, thus reinforcing our habits and perceptions. The expression 'You can't teach an old dog new tricks' is testament to this neurological fact.

So, to create a new 'habit' or 'perception' or 'behaviour', the 'new way' needs constant reinforcement and reminders and a multitude of stimuli all leading to the same destination. For example, hearing the same message said in different ways or by different people; experimenting, failing and trying again; seeing, hearing, touching – using all the senses; seeing it in others; not just reading it, but writing it, speaking it, doing it.

We then need repetition and reinforcement to enable that new way of learning to embed itself, to become a new, naturally stronger link – our new normality. Our mind is continually trying to readjust normality, though younger minds are more malleable. At night our dreams run through the day deciding which experiences are 'useful' to us and worth keeping. We filter all inputs and immediately discard what we perceive as not useful. The trouble here is that the filter operates at a subconscious level and is derived from past experiences, so to change our behaviour, we also need to challenge our filters. The power of your experience facilitates this embedding of the learning, challenging your filtering process and leading to long-lasting behavioural awareness and evolution.

I liken it to water flowing over the edge of a cliff. It has done so for millions of years and is comfortable in its laminar, or streamline, flow to the edge, in its smooth, well-worn and familiar channel. What we are trying to do here is to divert this stream to flow over another part of the cliff. We encourage it, put up barriers, dig new channels – all conscious actions. It flows, reluctantly at first, but it will follow our new path. However, it can, and will, easily revert to the old channel when the waters rise or the pressure comes back on. So we must encourage it and support it and 'remind' it about the 'new way' and rebuild the dams. Over time and with constant support the new channel becomes deeper than the old, and the old silts up and is forgotten. And so we adopt new thinking, new habits, new perceptions, new filters and new behaviours.

This book is designed to help us do just that. By sharing the learning through a story and matching an activity, the learning can be embedded.

Additionally, the brain rewards itself on creating new links. In our 'aha!' moments our brain releases endorphins into our bodies. These are natural opiates that 'reward' us for the learning. 'You cannot teach a man anything. You can only help him discover it within himself.' So said Galileo. Put another way, if you live your dreams and your words, it is within you, it is a part of you. But, if you try to live mine, it is outside of you – extrinsic, not owned by you – so those dreams, those words, are easily detached. We talk a lot later about 'finding the answer from within' when we look at coaching.

So, when I ask a question in this book, I urge you to answer it yourself before you read on. Stop and reflect. Think about it. Don't just skim over it. Make this book personal to you. Scribble on it. Use the notes section at the end of each chapter and at the back of the book set aside for your thinking. Use your words, your drawings, your interpretation and relate to your experiences. Then Galileo's thinking is applied. And the mere act of writing and translating adds more of those fatty links in the brain to the new model; and, when you then reread and apply what you have learned, so they become the new norm – the new natural way to lead. And how exciting is *that*!

Key Learnings

- UMU – this book is designed to be eminently useable, a practical guide and companion.

- Don't just rush through this book, when I ask you to stop and reflect – do so.

- The brain needs to create new links, many of them and repeatedly – read, write, experiment and reflect to keep up the experiences.

EXERCISE: WHAT'S YOUR STORY?

Storytelling is the most powerful way of sharing. It goes back to the dawn of man. It is deep within us, but, sadly, it has been beaten out of us over the years of operating in a highly directive corporate culture. But it is clear that the most compassionate, most impactful and most successful leaders I have met have been the storytellers.

So what is *your* story? I don't just mean a chronology of jobs, though you could start there if you wish, but what has been your emotional journey, what life events have left their mark, what has fashioned who you are now?

Here's what you must do. There are three parts to the exercise: the first two are personal; the other is about a style of communication.

I say that everybody has a story inside them. So, first, think about yours. What is it? Go on, write it down. Are there any key moments in your life that define you? Some key words perhaps? Try.

Next, think about how your story fits into the stories of the people around you. How does it fit into a bigger story? Who are the people around you? What is the bigger story?

And then finally, if you have a particular message you need to share with, say, your boss, colleagues, family, friends or ⟶

team, consider how you might use a story to get your point across. This could be a personal story, a well-known fable or parable, or another person's story. It doesn't matter, as long as it is a story, not an instruction.

Here are some examples in the grid below:

Whom am I trying to share with?	What is my message?	What story could I use?
My boss	That if they listened more to the ideas from the team, we might find a better solution and we would get more commitment.	'Hi Boss, I need to share something. The other day as I was in the coffee queue ...' Or: 'I was reading a book on great leaders in history by ...'
My son	Please don't drop your clothes on the floor.	'When I was a lad ...' 'When Apollo 13 failed to land on the moon, the astronaut could not find his trousers ...'

Notes

_____

_____

_____

_____

_____

_____

_____

_____

CHAPTER 3

_____

KEY THINKING

If you took my advice earlier, you'll have jumped to this chapter before reading the one about how the book works. You need to read this bit first, because it's the big picture, the context. Understand this, and rest will follow. But, hey, if you read the previous chapter first, then that's cool too!

This is where you will learn the fundamental principles of my thinking, which are different and challenging. This book is a perspective on life and leadership fashioned from myriads of experiences and conversations – fashioned not just by my actions and expeditions, but equally by my interactions and dialogues with the players and leaders across the business and sporting worlds, my children and the children I coach, and the people, from all walks of life, who have shared their story with me. Each time I engage in 'leadership development' for people, it is equally part of my own leadership-development journey. Consider this a collective wisdom, and, if you have been on one of my courses or at one of my lectures, or part of my adventures, or shared your story, then thank you for your insights and feedback, for, as I am sure you know well, the best way to learn is to teach!

I am keen to share upfront my thinking on the words _leadership_ and _relationship_ and how they go together.

Leadership, relationship and high performance

Having an understanding of what it takes to form lasting relationships and how to engage individuals to reach solutions is an essential ability for a Compassionate Leader. Making things happen for other people is what drives me forward, and this involves an active focus on relationship development. It has taken me many years and a plethora of adventures to be able to put into words what I have seen, felt and experienced.

Whenever I am asked to talk on the subject of leadership, I open by challenging the very word. Even using the word *leadership* brings with it limiting beliefs and disengagement. It causes misunderstanding and fear. People have a tendency to think, Hey, it's not for me: it's for those above me. That is wrong! It is for everyone. You start by leading yourself. But, most importantly, you then need to be able to *relate* to others in order to *lead* others. Leadership, unfortunately, is a term that evokes a feeling of hierarchy and prestige. To me, a leader is only as good as the relationships that they form, and the word *relationship* is far more profound than *leadership*.

Compassionate Leadership is about people as individuals, thinking of a team as a collection of diverse and complementary members with differing needs, wants and emotional requirements. It is about a 'collective intelligence', inspiring ideas, motivation and actions, and fulfilling people's lives.

Compassionate Leadership is 'relationship', in the context of achieving a collective task.

Leaders are frequently faced with demanding, high-pressure situations and so, for longevity of leadership to exist, for sustained high performance and to create a committed – as opposed to merely compliant – team, a leader must have formed lasting, trusting relationships. I say 'Give me a motivated team of developed individuals and I will achieve any task!' However, there will, on occasions, despite the proverbial best-laid schemes, be situations when a task starts to become hard as a multitude of internal and external factors outside of anyone's control begin to play a hand, and it is then that valued relationships and the resultant commitment of team members play their part. It is the early 'hard yards' in building the relationship and trust that will pay dividends later.

Research supports the concept that the skills involved in relationships form the major elements of the skills required for leadership. An in-depth study on high-performance organisations (HPOs) carried out by the Dutch business theorist Professor André de Waal clearly demonstrates that for an organisation to be high-performing there are 35 'characteristics of high performance' that need to be developed and maintained; 27 of these are about the quality of people and the quality of relationships; 77 per cent of the time and effort, skills and focus, energy and knowledge of a leader needs to be focused on developing people – including oneself – and relationships.

And the benefits of being an HPO are extraordinary. According to de Waal's research, for organisations that score well across the HPO factors, it has been empirically shown that:

- revenue growth increases by 4% to 16%
- profitability increases by 14% to 44%
- return on assets (ROA) increases by 1% to 12%
- return on equity (ROE) increases by 9% to 25%
- return on investment (ROI) increases by 15% to 26%
- return on sales (ROS) increases by 2% to 18%
- total shareholder return increases by 4% to 42%

In the area of non-financial performance HPOs repeat this feat. They achieve much higher:

- non-financial benefits
- customer satisfaction
- customer loyalty
- employee satisfaction
- innovation (quality and renewal)

And that is with two-thirds of your effort, your leadership effort, being on the 'people' bit, the relationship bit.

Thus, this book is essentially about relationship development, and the skills and principles discussed can be applied in all life situations: at work, at home, with friends, with kids – anywhere a relationship is needed.

As a leader, consider yourself first as a 'relater'.

So what is the outcome of Compassionate Leadership? The outcome within the team, the people you are influencing, leading? The outcome for yourself?

It is about getting the job done, of course. But, to get the job done, do you need a 'committed' or a 'compliant' team or individual? I refer to this throughout the book. I would argue that, in all life's situations, it becomes easier, more effective, higher-performing and a lot more fun if there is the commitment to the cause – this is also a key premise of Compassionate Leadership.

Commitment vs compliance

Let's dwell a moment on this difference between commitment and mere compliance. There is always an outcome of our inter-action or relationship with another person. We have the ability to solicit two responses. A person can be either committed to our influence and desires, or just compliant. There is a third response of course, that of refusal, but we can talk more about that at another time, and I guess all refusal is really a lack of either commitment or compliance.

I touched above on the idea of a committed, as opposed to a compliant, team. To me there is a gaping, icy crevasse of difference between the two. Think how you feel when you are merely complying with a task.

Stop reading this for a moment and reflect on what the emotions are within you when you are compliant with a task. Write the emotions down. Go on.

You may feel your energy being sapped; you may feel bored,

defensive; you may find yourself providing poor-quality work, wishing to work elsewhere; maybe time drags, and you're frustrated and annoyed.

These emotions are real to you and to the people around you, and impact not just on behaviour but on the intrinsic motivation that *drives* behaviour. Look at the people you lead. Are they compliant with your wishes? Are energy and passion low? Think of the cost to you and your business. Is constant supervision required? Do all decisions come to the top? Is no one taking responsibility or initiative? Do you detect poor performance?

Now think about how you feel when you are committed to a task. Again, stop reading for a moment. Actually reflect how it feels when you are committed to a task. Write it down.

You want to do it. You feel energised, excited, dedicated, keen to do the best you can. Time flies, you feel motivated.

If you can get your team to be committed to their task, to their fellow team members and to your vision, think of the impact this would have. You have more time to do your job and the team are empowered and motivated, giving you a better return on your investment in them as a whole – reaping both financial and human advantages. And, suddenly, people begin to smile. Their internal, intrinsic motivation kicks in and they are up and running.

But there is a tension within this, as I discovered while facilitating a debate on the subject with a roomful of business leaders. It's a funny story, actually, if you picture the scene.

I was asking how people feel about being compliant with the job in hand, and the answers included words such as *reluctant*, *bored*, *frustrated*. Then a voice from the back of the room shouted out, 'Relieved.' I ignored it and moved on. 'So, tell me what it feels like when you're committed to a task.' Among the words that came back to me were *excited*, *enthusiastic* and *passionate*. Then the same voice from the back of the room piped up saying, 'Stressed.' This time I could not ignore the person.

The whole room was looking at him and looking back at me to see what I would do. This person was known to be a 'challenge'. So I asked him, 'Sorry, could you explain? Your thinking is contrary to what I was expecting.'

And I am so glad I did ask and not dismiss, for the answer has stuck with me and was a big lesson learned. 'Well,' our protagonist replied, 'if I have to do stuff and I am compliant with it, I don't care about it. I just turn up, get it done, and head home again. But, if I'm committed to it, I'm really keen to get it right, I want it to be perfect and that stresses me out.'

Superb! What a great lesson! Thank you. There is a responsibility when we strive to create a 'committed' team in that, with that commitment comes pressure and potentially stress. Likewise, with compliance comes a complete disengagement and potential internal conflict as self-worth is lost. And you must be cognisant of both.

But here's the rub, the Big Understanding, if you like: leaders create commitment; leaders also create compliance. (By the way, this is the same with parents.) Leaders create the culture that is in front of them. If that is an environment where people sit back rather than step forward, a culture where people are not taking initiative, an ethos of high absence and low productivity, it is because of the leader. The leader created it. You created it. No externalising. No excuses.

But there is good news. Once a leader understands the impact of their behaviour, they can choose to change it. They can choose a behaviour that creates a culture of committed teams and lasting relationships. It is within the control of the leader to change.

So, are you up for it? When you as a leader see a 'compliant' team or individual, say to yourself, '*I* created that – and how does that make me feel?' Because they will be feeling the same. Likewise, you create commitment, so say the same: 'I created that committed, driven, motivated and happy team. Well done, me!' And they will see and feel that pride.

Key Learnings

- Leadership is relationship – but with common endeavour; to lead you will need to relate.

- High Performance Organisation research reveals that we need to spend roughly ⅔rds of our time ($^{27}/_{35}$ths to be precise) developing the quality of our people, ourselves and our relationships.

- Working to gain Commitment pays massive dividends over forcing Compliance – think about the ROI.

EXERCISE: COMMITMENT VS COMPLIANCE

For the second activity, let's look at the impact of commitment or compliance on ourselves first, then I will ask you to reflect on the 'mood' of your team.

You will need to ask these questions:

- What emotions arise within you if you are asked to do a job that you don't believe in, don't particularly want to do, but know you have to do?

- What emotions arise within in you when you embark upon a task that you love, that you own and that you know will make a difference?

Make two lists. Use emotional words. Let it flow.

Hold these emotions in your mind as you consider the next question, which is whether you believe your team are in a compliant or committed state. And, whatever the outcome of your deliberations, remember that a leader creates the team they deserve. A tad harsh, to be honest, as there are many other factors too, but, as a Compassionate Leader, you must not shy away from your responsibilities. Whenever I have struggled ➡

with a team, I consider their mood and then look at what I have done to create that mood.

Be brutally honest as you try to decide whether they're merely compliant or truly committed. If need be, go and ask. Do not write what you want, but write what is.

With each team or group, try to break it down into subgroups or individuals, depending on the scale of your organisation.

If you see 'commitment', write down why you believe that and what you are going to do to maintain that. If you see 'compliance', again, write down why you believe that and what you are going to do to help them break out of that. Use the example grid below to help.

Team	Committed or compliant	Evidence	My action
Ops team	Compliant	I have to work really hard to make sure stuff gets done. Quiet office, no one really smiles. Work quality not great.	Have a one-to-one with the team leader to get their point of view. Have a team meeting to listen to their concerns. Create a 'dialogue' around your strategic thinking.
Sales team	Committed	There is a buzz in their office. They are selling, but, even if they miss their figures, they still go straight back out with more drive.	Have a one-to-one with the team leader to get their point of view. Learn what is making the team tick. Possibly engage them with the ops team to share best practice.

The investment

If you are too busy to delegate correctly, too busy to create a sense of purpose, too busy or afraid to seek feedback or suggestions, too busy to get that commitment and buy-in, then you create compliance. If you direct, tell, instruct, force, coerce, then compliance is the likely response. The initiative and decision making have to stay with you. The ideas have to come from you. Your supervision is needed constantly – you become a 'busy fool'. Your investment in effort to stand still will need to increase over time.

It isn't just the emotion associated with compliance that you have created within the team or individual. It is also the *cost* of compliance to your organisation: poor productivity, high staff turnover, high absenteeism, customer dissatisfaction, disengagement and more. And the cost of compliance on you: stress, short-term priorities, being too busy to think, frustration and a negative impact on your work–life balance. And the cost of compliance to your family: rebellious teenagers, reluctant partner, arguments and dysfunction. Ouch! Can you afford compliance?

So just before you task your team or an individual, stop. Invest the effort to create purpose, agree a plan, engage with their collective brilliance, understand their concerns and thoughts, gain their commitment to the action. In other words, delegate correctly, empower your people and enjoy their commitment and enjoy the *benefits* of commitment – the time invested early creates an ROI many times larger – you gain time – the area under the graph! Time you can use to actually be a 'leader', and not just a busy, stressed manager.

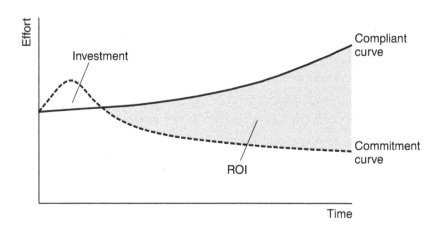

Figure 3.1 Commitment vs compliance

The area under the graph shows that the initial early investment reaps massive returns later on. A disempowered or
disengaged team will be compliant and need increased management and supervision – you will become increasingly busy
standing still! An early investment to gain commitment gives
a healthy return in the effort, initiative and productivity of
your team.

But this takes 'courage'! One of those 'Big Five' values we
spoke about at the beginning. The courage to stop before you
start. The courage to make that early investment. This is a
theme that is repeated throughout this book!

From this point on you may read this book in any order you
wish, so long as you have read this bit first. Or you can go back
to where we 'left off' in Chapter 2.

Not everyone likes to follow the rules and read a book
front to back. (I know I don't.) So go with your intuition and
read how you want to read. If you have a specific problem
that you would like to resolve, then whisk yourself to the part
that is most useful to you. Feel free to learn as you wish to
learn.

I have included space at the end of each chapter for you to

add your notes and thoughts. Use this to anchor your learning. Add your experiences to my experiences and thoughts and then we can create a collective brilliance. Also, you can share your thinking and your stories with me and your input to our collective leadership journey can be incorporated in future editions. Put your thoughts on the book's associated blog which can be found at www.manleytalks.com/compassion).

Enjoy and learn – enjoyment and learning go hand in hand; I believe there is no other way! Add joy to everything that you do: remember, it's not just about work, it's about all life situations.

Notes

_____

_____

_____

_____

_____

_____

_____

_____

_____

_____

_____

CHAPTER 4

SO WHAT IS IT, AND WHY?

Compassionate Leadership – a definition

Before we get bogged down discussing exactly what Compassionate Leadership is, let's take a look at the reason for it, since from the outcome comes the definition.

What is the effect? The outcome? It is an interesting question that I have asked many groups. Once we strip away the skills of leadership and the behaviours, attributes and values and start to focus on *why* we need leadership, it becomes clear. Stripped down to its barest form, the output of leadership is getting others to do stuff! To collectively get stuff done. But Compassionate Leadership is so much more than that. The neatest articulation of the outcome or definition of Compassionate Leadership came recently from a leadership workshop I was giving with a group of leaders in a large IT company.

It was:

'**To secure the best for, and the best out of, your people, your organisation, your stakeholders and yourself.**'

I like this definition a lot. This is my reason for being. It sums up Compassionate Leadership very well indeed.

It is not just securing the best *out of* someone, but also the best *for* the person; not just the best *out of* the organisation, but the best *for* it, and so on, for all the stakeholders.

Compassionate Leadership is not just about shareholder return. Nor is it just about the team or the leader, or any individual component. Nor is it just about you! It is for all.

This is a key premise of Compassionate Leadership. Leadership is about legacy as much as it is about action. Compassionate Leadership is about motivation as much as it is about direction. It is about stewardship as much as it is about ownership. It is a balance.

Let's break the definition down.

'To secure the best for and out of all.'

To 'secure' something is more than just 'getting' or 'obtaining' it. It has become something that is solid, dependable, firm. If something is secure, I can rely on it, lean on it, trust it. It takes effort to secure something. You have to make something secure.

Leadership is not just about getting stuff out of someone: it is also about doing stuff *for* that someone, about putting stuff back in. We can demand an 'out of' or manage an 'out of'; they are both short-term and, as we will discuss later, likely to lead to compliance, not commitment. No, leadership is both: yes, it is about getting stuff done, or *out of*, but it is also about putting back or doing stuff *for*. That way, we create a sustainable and growing engagement with a coherent commitment to what needs to be done.

How do you feel when you have done something for someone? How do you feel when someone else has done something for you? How do you feel when you have helped someone be the best they can be? And how do you feel when someone else has helped you perform? These are the emotions associated with Compassionate Leadership.

Leadership is about achievement, legacy and growth. Securing the best out of your people makes sense in achieving the task. Securing the best for your people is all about development, long-term achievement and intrinsic motivation. Developing your people allows you to move on; you cannot move up and leave a vacuum behind you. Developing your people enables them to add greater value; you can achieve so much more with more capable people. Developing your people creates commitment and the realisation of an effective power base (see Chapter 7, 'Who Gives the Power?').

As for your organisation, clearly, to ensure the best *for* it and the best *out of* it is a no-brainer. Through your organisation you can achieve. A successful organisation can grow, change, develop and be secure. A successful organisation provides opportunity and security – two basic elements of intrinsic motivation. A leader needs their organisation to work for them and they need to work for it too. A high-performing organisation is fun to be in and prosperous.

Your stakeholders are not just shareholders, but all those with an interest in your success: family, friends, investors, customers, your boss, your team, your peers, the planet. I add 'the planet' deliberately, as it ties in with the concept of stewardship. We may well be the dominant species at the moment, but that does not give us the right to abuse the planet or other sentient beings. So one of the stakeholders of a Compassionate Leader is the planet itself. A Compassionate Leader needs not only to secure the best out of the resources the planet offers, and that must be done for most efficient use of finite resources, but a Compassionate Leader must also secure the best *for* the planet! A Compassionate Leader understands their responsibility to *all* stakeholders – and that includes future generations of our own species and others.

To explain why this is so important I would like to share the thinking of a good friend and a great inspiration, Kate Chapman. Kate has been advising global organisations including the Olympic Committee on how to make sustainability real, how we can and must create a symbiotic balance between the economy and society.

Kate's thinking is another key premise of compassionate leadership and is about the balance and focus for the three interdependent elements of *economy, society* and *ecosystem.* For true sustainability it is vital that the *economy* must serve *society* so that *society* can serve the *ecosystem* – that way all is in harmony and balance.

Today, it seems that the *economy* is serving fewer and fewer in *society* and that society is actually serving the *economy* and so forgetting or unable to fulfill its responsibility to its *ecosystem* – with the impact of this clear in environmental disasters and societal stress. A Compassionate Leader strives for balance.

Clearly, all your stakeholders create demands on you: they want your time, your effort, your input, your thoughts. However, to be truly effective, it is vital that you also get the best out of them, too. They are, after all, your support network.

Then, last but definitely not least, there's your own self. You need to secure the best out of and for yourself. There is no sustainability of longevity in leadership if you are not able to give of your best, or, in the process, you are not able to get the best for yourself. This is so important to understand. If your future is not aligned to that of your organisation, how can you be committed to it? If you cannot see your goal or the steps of your life's journey within the goals of where you work, how can you fulfil your self-worth? More about that when we talk about commitment.

Leadership vs relationship (revisited)

So how are you going to secure the best for and from your people, your organisation, your stakeholders and yourself? What's going to make the difference? Let's look at that business of leadership versus relationship again, and, indeed, try using the word *relationship* instead of *leadership*.

As I said in Chapter 3, in my experience, using the word *leadership* brings with it limiting beliefs and disengagement.

I believe there are a number of disconnects about what is expected of a leader and who should be leading. If we're lower down in the organisation, then, when we hear the word *leadership*, we think, Well, it's not for me: it's for those in the top of the organisation. If we're at the top of the organisation, there's a feeling of, Well, I have that skill anyway, or I wouldn't be at the top. So the audience limit their ability to absorb the new learning. They are limiting their beliefs, limiting their engagement and limiting their ability to lead.

I often hear leaders say, 'I would never ask anyone to do anything that I wouldn't do myself.' This thinking is fundamentally flawed. It's OK, in principle, in some respects, such as the number of hours or amount of effort one puts in. For instance, if I want my team to work weekends or late, then I should be prepared to do so, too. But the whole point of a team is to bring people together who have a variety of skills and experiences, so the collective brilliance outshines the individual. There is no way that I can do what most of my team are capable of doing! That is not my job.

The word *leader* conjures up images of great individual heroics. Some think of leadership as a 'Charge! Follow me, men, over the top!' type of activity. And, yes, when times are tough or when you're going into battle, that is leadership – leading from the front.

How the leader acts when the going gets tough is important for confidence in the moment, but the real work of leadership, the effort that reaps great rewards, is in the building of relationships before the cannons roar. Admiral Horatio Nelson's leadership in the Battle of Trafalgar was not that influential: he was dead for most of it! He would have been no good up the rigging anyway: he only had one arm and one eye! Nelson's great skill and his biggest impact were not in the heat of this particular battle, but in the relationships he had developed before with his Band of Brothers (as he called his captains) and all of his sailors. Their commitment and motivation in serving the needs of their leader was less to do with the moment than how he related to them and they to him. Nelson was different. He understood his men and went beyond the leadership style of the period to look after his men and truly get to know them. Even when blockading the French and Spanish fleets in their Mediterranean ports, he developed a network of 'friendly' harbours and suppliers on foreign soil that enabled him to provide for his men. He walked with them without fear for his own security and he treated them fairly.

The most important part of Compassionate Leadership is done way before the battle. Once it's begun, it's too late to start creating concepts of relationship and trust. So, when we talk about how to be a leader, I want you to understand that Compassionate Leadership, at its core, comes from relationship.

Great Scott

Let me share with you my interpretation of the leadership of Captain Robert Falcon Scott, and how it was his relationship with and understanding of his men that enabled them to achieve what even his explorer rival Roald Amundsen did not. I would like to add my weight in support of Scott.

A lot has been written about that other polar explorer Ernest Shackleton and about what a superb leader *he* was. There is no doubt that he was, indeed, one of the world's greatest leaders. His determination to keep his men alive was extraordinary, and, if you have not read of him, I urge you to do so. Throughout his battles, Nelson was always the first to tell his story and write history. And so it was with Shackleton. He survived so he could tell his own story. Sadly, this was not to be for Scott. Shackleton's story is one of heroics and life, whereas Scott's is one of heroics and death.

Roland Huntford wrote a book on Scott that paints him as an arrogant buffoon, as someone who wouldn't take dogs, essentially wouldn't trust or listen to his men, who had issues 'relating' to his men (and the wider society). Unfortunately, this book became the basis of the modern thinking on Scott as a leader and was interpreted in film. Even a recent sketch on the children's television programme *Horrible Histories* painted the picture so. However, let me share with you this one story that I think challenges that view, and is part of what my polar expeditions were about. (Though I know I am no Scott and make no such arrogant pretensions.)

Scott had travelled to Antarctica to undertake a three-year expedition of scientific discovery and exploration, and it was also a case of 'While you're there, Scott, claim the Pole for Britain'; he was there to finish the job so nearly done by Shackleton in his 1909 expedition, retrospectively dubbed the 'furthest South'. Thanks to the efforts of Nelson 100 years before, we actually had an empire and that brought with it a confidence – some would say arrogance – that Britain could do anything and that there were no other nations out there prepared or able to undertake such an audacious endeavour as to claim the South Pole. Indeed, publicly, at that time, both the USA and Norway in particular were challenging for the North Pole, and Amundsen, when he left Norway, had declared to the world that he was going north. His team thought he was, the world thought he was – but it was to be a deliberate decoy. It was only when he got to Madeira that Amundsen briefed his men on his real intention, then sent a signal to the king of Norway to say he was going south to claim the South Pole for Norway. By the time the message had got through to Scott he did not have the time to react. Scott was never built for speed, but for scientific survey, study and understanding, and claiming the Pole for Britain was to be just one part of a larger project.

It was also always about *man's* endeavour to get to the South Pole, not the wind's or an animal's, but the ingenuity, determination, skill and effort of man at his best. Amundsen, on the other hand, *was* built for speed. His intention was to beat Scott, to get to the South Pole first, no matter how. This is not a critique of Amundsen but just a demonstration of the difference in thinking and hence the inequity of a 'race' that, in essence, was never a race.

Picture the scene. You are Scott. It is late summer and the sun is no longer high in the sky, but just hovers on the horizon. The time is creeping closer to when the sun will not show its face again for three months, when the darkness and ferocity of an Antarctic winter tighten their grip on all. Having survived the savage cold, in the spring you'll be heading to claim the Pole, to go further than anyone has gone before, deep within the interior of Antarctica, battling the harshest continent to its very heart. A group of your men are surveying the coastline of the Ross Ice Shelf, and they bump into the Norwegians. No one knows they're there. Suddenly they see a tent and think, Who's that? They get closer and see five Norwegians and a pack of dogs; the Norwegians have set up camp on the ice some 120 miles closer to the South Pole. With a team of just five people and with 45 dogs to pull them on their way, their intent is clear. The Norwegian team is set up for speed. They ooze confidence and familiarity.

They say, 'Scott, yah! We'll beat you to the Pole in the spring.'

Your men travel back as fast as they can in the fading light, battling hard with doubt gnawing in their hearts. They rehearse how they are to break the news. In the enforced isolation of protective clothing, as the winds bite, so their hopes fade. Exhausted, a week later they arrive back at your camp to be cheered, but then there is silence as they share their story: 'The Norwegians are in Antarctica. They are closer to the Pole. They have dogs. They will beat us to the Pole. All is lost.'

The winter is harsh and long. There is no other place on this planet with conditions as violent as Antarctica. The sun has gone, clear nights bring with them an abundance of stars but bone-numbing chill. Then the stars are blanked out by the driven snow and ice, and the howling winds can reach over 200 miles an hour, threatening to sweep all before them with a destructive force unparalleled on Earth. To survive an Antarctic winter is a feat in itself, but to focus your mind and spend your time thinking beyond the dark in preparing and planning for your assault on the centre demonstrates the incredible power of the human spirit when inspired by a vision.

Through this time, Scott kept his men focused, motivated, fit, prepared, organised and balanced. Not a moment was wasted. Each day added value to the spring's endeavour. All effort was in preparation, so when they left as the sun rose, optimistic externally, they knew deep inside that, save for misfortune for the Norwegians, they would not get to the Pole first. But such was their total motivation and commitment, inspired by Scott's vision, example and leadership, that the men were happy to accompany their leader even to their own death.

History will tell you that Amundsen and his team were the first men to reach the South Pole. That is true. But Scott and his team were the first men to reach the South Pole under man's efforts alone – unsupported and unassisted.

If that isn't leadership, tell me what leadership really is. It was not just how Scott led in the heat of the moment (if that's not a totally inappropriate expression to use in these circumstances!): it was the trust and relationships that he built up in the months and years before hitting the ice that allowed him to achieve what no man, not even Amundsen, had achieved before. He was so close to being able to tell his own story, but, with injury and unseasonably poor weather, that was not to be. We will never know what it was like. We can try to empathise, to put ourselves in their shoes, but I would not dare to presume. When I do eventually go south, the world will be a very different place than it was in Scott's time.

To lead compassionately is to relate. How you respond when the going gets tough is important, but, for the team to follow you no matter what, you need more than heroics of the moment. You need to have spent time gaining their absolute trust, respect and loyalty, as Captain Robert Falcon Scott most certainly did. To know your people deeply, to understand their needs, desires, wants, skills, concerns, motivations, weaknesses and so forth, demands that you build relationships; it demands that you be a Compassionate Leader.

Think back to my thoughts on commitment versus compliance in Chapter 3. It is the behaviour of the leader that creates a committed team. It is the behaviour of the leader that creates a compliant team.

So, in introducing my talks I say, 'Rather than talk about "motivational leadership", I'm going to talk about "motivational relationship" or "relationships in troubled waters" – in other words, "Compassionate Leadership"!'

For Captain Scott's men, the direction and support were there in spades; the whole team's competence and commitment were absolute. But Scott also had the understanding and ability to be the facilitator of ideas and allowed his men great freedom in providing the solutions. He *knew* his men absolutely, and it was this relationship knowledge that made the difference.

So let's look at what it all means.

Yourself, your people, your stakeholders

Let's look at self-leadership first. How can I secure the best *for* me if I do not know what it is I need and want? How can I secure the best *out of* me if I do not know what it is I can do best?

And what of my team and other stakeholders? How can I secure the best *for* someone if I do not know what it is they need? How can I secure the best *out of* someone if I do not know what they can do?

Through leading yourself, you are getting yourself to do something. But, when leading teams and other people, you are trying to get them to achieve something collectively, to achieve something maybe they wouldn't have done before, to achieve something you want to be done. In other words, leadership is about influencing others.

It could be with my team on a sporting pitch. They're behind, the clock is ticking away and I'm trying to influence them to dig deep and turn the game around so we can win it. I may be trying to influence colleagues in a business, a boardroom or an organisation to go the extra mile, to do more than they thought they could do. I need to influence people through times when it's tough, secure the best out of people and secure their commitment to what needs to happen. Or it could be in the home and I want to influence my children, what they do with their life, what values they think are important.

To influence, to lead in any of these situations, requires that I relate to the people involved.

Think about what relationship actually is. Relationship is about influencing somebody, whether it's your loved one, your sporting team, your offspring, your peers or your boss. If you can relate to them – and by that I mean understand them and they can understand you – and if you can build an element of trust and loyalty, then the skills of leadership that you need to apply to get people to do what you want become so much easier to use.

Compassionate Leadership is relationship, but in the context of a common endeavour.

Compassionate Leadership is about maximising relationships to achieve a collective intelligence; it's about inspiring ideas, motivation and actions and fulfilling people's lives. When leading a team, think about people as individuals, and of a team as a collection of diverse and complementary people with differing needs, wants and emotional requirements. Relate to them. Be compassionate.

Friendship!

Just to clarify, relationship does not mean friendship. I do not have to like you or enjoy your company to relate to you. Think of Nelson and his Band of Brothers. He did not always enjoy their presence, but he knew them, respected them and created a relationship that allowed him to secure the *best out of* and *best for* them all, himself and his major stakeholder – Britain.

To create a relationship, I do not have to be chummy. I do not have to socialise if I do not care to. But I must invest the time to create the relationship. And, conversely, how can I even consider creating a friendship if I cannot develop a relationship?

This all links sweetly to my understanding of emotional intelligence, the way your knowledge of yourself, of others and of the environment you create allows the relationship to develop. I have captured this in an UMU (understandable, memorable, usable) model – which I call Me, You and Us – in the next chapter.

Think about all the great leaders in your own life – people who have inspired you, or people you would follow to the end of the world. What was it about them? Go on, make a note about that person and why you considered them to be an inspiring leader. When you reflect and move on from the value-type words we shared earlier, it will be because you felt you could relate to them; they had your best interests at heart; they were trying to secure the best for and from you; they were 'relaters'. In short, they were Compassionate Leaders.

When the winds are fair and it is all plain sailing, leadership is relatively easy, because, when the pressure is off, motivation is not the issue. But what happens when the winds howl and the waves grow? When things start to go wrong? When you need to recover from failure or loss? When the team starts falling apart and tensions rise? That is when you reap what you have sown. That is when the investment you have made in building relationships, developing trust and truly knowing your people, and they you, pays off. That is when the relationship side of leadership comes to the fore. It is at this time that an understanding of the differing motivational drivers of your team members makes the difference between success and failure, between recovery and further decline.

Compassionate Leadership demands you 'know' yourself and your people.

Key Learnings

- Compassionate leadership is 'to secure the best for and out of all'.

- We must balance the relationship so that the *economy* serves *society* that serves the *ecosystem*.

- Nelson and Scott both 'knew' their men. They gained great loyalty through their "compassionate leadership".

- It all starts with 'leading self – that's you!

EXERCISE: REFLECTION ON LEADERSHIP

The exercise associated with this chapter is one of reflection. Consider the people you lead. What sort of relationship do you have with them? Do you actually know them? Are you getting the best *for* them and are you getting the best *out of* them? Don't just think it: write down your observations. Own the observations.

Consider your style of leadership. Does it foster relationships, or does it keep everyone at arm's length?

Try to use the 'thinking' and 'emotion' of relationship as opposed to the 'corporate expectation' of traditional directive leadership.

Remember, to build a relationship with someone is not the same as being a best mate! It is about understanding and respect!

Notes

_____

_____

_____

_____

_____

_____

_____

_____

CHAPTER 5

ME, YOU AND US

It is clear from all the leaders I have met over the years that it is those with the greater sense of self-awareness who achieve more. Their heightened self-awareness allows them to fully understand the impact they have on others; it enables them to develop a greater sense of empathy and to be able to modify their behaviour accordingly, thus creating the environment for success.

In essence, this is about *emotional intelligence*, or EI. It is at the core of all relationship development and hence leadership, too. It is at the heart of Compassionate Leadership.

A lot of very good books (and some very long ones) have been written about EI, and, in line with my UMU principle and a desire to help the application of EI for the benefit of all leaders (and relaters), I have naturally simplified the concept.

I have spent a lot of time working with different groups of people – be they business or sporting or expedition teams – trying to make emotional intelligence accessible. I believe I have done so – in a simplified form, but nonetheless in a form that we can use. My model and interpretation is just that: an understandable, memorable and usable interpretation of the theory of EI. I have deliberately used simple words.

The diagram opposite represents the central premise of my Me, You and Us model.

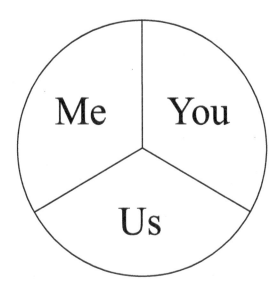

Figure 5.1 Me, You and Us

Knowing me, knowing you, knowing us

In this chapter, we'll explore the idea of fostering the desire to know more about 'me'. We'll strive to understand 'you', and we'll create the constructive environment that allows 'us' to grow and develop.

Knowing me

Why is 'knowing me' so important?

One of the basic premises of mankind, as expressed in Jungian thinking, is that we are all trying to fulfil the universal goal of self-worth. Self-worth comes from self-respect and self-esteem. It is a constant within us all and our only way to true contentment. We do things to make ourselves feel good, not bad. Even someone stealing your car is not trying to make themselves feel bad!

As the American psychologist Elias Porter (1914–87) describes it in his excellent work accessed through his Strength

Deployment Inventory (a superbly UMU tool that I thoroughly recommend), not to fulfil self-worth creates inner conflict, and inner conflict tends to polarise our behaviour in an emotional and irrational way. It greatly impacts on our ability to relate to others. Let's look at the two elements of self-worth: self-respect and self-esteem. Self-respect comes from doing things that we value ourselves for; we want to do that which makes us feel good. We are instinctively motivated to act in a way that fills us with self-respect. We gain self-respect by doing things that are true to our real self.

Self-esteem is being valued by others for doing things that we value ourselves for. How can you compliment me unless you know me? How can I receive an intended compliment if I do not know myself?

Together, it's all about self-worth.

Clearly, if we're going to try to tap into and build our self-respect, we have to know ourselves. We have to know what is important to us, what our values are, our motivations and needs, our strengths.

When I have this conversation with people in various walks of life, I ask, 'How can we commit to an organisation if we don't know ourselves?' If I don't know me, how can I match my needs to those of any organisation or group? How do I know I will fit in? How do I know that it will fulfil my needs? How do I know that my goals are being met? We discuss this more in Chapter 9, which is all about creating the culture associated with Compassionate Leadership.

Putting these thoughts together, we see that we need to create what I call a *conscious compromise*. Let me explain.

There is an old Jesuit saying: 'Give me a child for his first seven years, and I will give you the man.' (Language was more male-oriented when that was written, so bear in mind that this applies equally well to women.) This is all about those early life experiences being so formative. The diagram opposite shows what I mean very well.

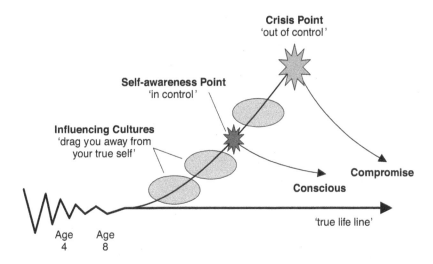

Figure 5.2 The conscious compromise curve

> Don't work toward freedom, but allow the work
> itself to be freedom.
>
> – Dogen Roshi, Rinzai Zen Buddhist monk

It is in the first four years of our lives that we really work out who we are. Our ego develops once we realise we are separate from our mothers and is used as a defence mechanism in helping us relate to the world. We refine this in the next three to five years, so, when we are eight, our values are pretty much set and what should happen is that we live our lives true to our value set – we fulfil our self-worth.

I saw this next part in my own children. Up to about eight years old, they responded in ways that were true to themselves, true to their own character and value set. We say it is 'sweet' and 'naïve' but we all coo when a small child responds not as society would expect, but as they see the world. Then, at around eight, a tragedy unfolds. Instead of responding true to themselves, they start to realise that they are being judged. The free thinking is replaced by a qualified response formed by their asking, What is expected of me? How should I respond? Depending on the dominant cultures that they find themselves in, children no longer respond true to themselves but true to the culture of the situation. They start the journey away from their own true life's path, away from their value set, and move steadily further away from being able to fulfil self-worth. They become aware of the dominant cultures of our society, of school, peer expectation, strong media influence and the corporate world. As they march through life, at a conscious or an unconscious level, they find themselves being less and less true to themselves. They lose the ability to fulfil self-worth. They have lost their inner self.

Eventually, this inner conflict is too much. They snap. They grow their hair, get a tattoo and drive a Harley-Davidson. It's a midlife crisis as they try to live as that eight-year-old kid used to be, as they try to fulfil self-worth. (Apologies if you have a Harley! Only an image, not a reality – I love them.)

We see this everywhere in society as our inner discontentment spills out into our behaviour: road rage, depression, anger, stress.

So let's change that image. Instead of going to 'crisis point', let's create an 'awareness point'. Let us truly discover who we are. Remind ourselves of that eight-year-old kid we used to be. What was our value set then, for it will be pretty much the same now? But we cannot become that eight-year-old child any more. Our lives have moved on; we will have responsibilities and a need to relate to our society. But what we can do is create a 'conscious compromise'. We can be aware of who we really are, raise our awareness of what space we are playing in at the moment, what we are doing, and create a 'conscious compromise' that we can be happy with.

Self-worth fulfilled, inner conflict removed, emotions and behaviour under our control. By raising our 'knowing me' awareness, we:

- have that chance to fulfil **self-worth** at a conscious level and remove potential inner conflict

- are able to behave towards the **best outcome** in any situation
- can **match our activity** to our needs and skills
- can **commit** to an organisation
- can **relate** to others
- can **start the journey** to becoming a Compassionate Leader

What do you need to know of yourself? And why?

These two powerful questions can form the core of a whole conference. I frequently ask them of people as the starter to self-discovery, either within a personal-coaching environment or as a team. The answers reveal so much about ourselves, and our culture, in both the words people say and the words they struggle with.

Over the years, these are the words that have come back in response to the first question, 'What do you need to know of yourself?'

Your name (Ha!), strengths and weaknesses, limits, motivations, goals, needs, beliefs, values, priorities, presumptions, prejudices, experiences, behaviours, character, emotions . . . And there are variations on the themes. These exact words are not critical in themselves, and you may well have produced another list; but, when you reach for your thesaurus, you'll find yourself in this ballpark.

Infrequently volunteered but always enticed are two critical facets of character that we most certainly need to know: how we are perceived by others, and our emotions.

So let's go through the list above and see how important they are, and why.

Strengths

Absolutely crucial. We must play to our strengths. That is where we can add the most value and gain the most satisfaction. I generally find that these also link very closely to the things I enjoy doing; I am definitely better at doing the stuff I enjoy. But do you know your strengths? Go on, list them now. Many people find it very hard to articulate what their strengths actually are, and almost impossible to share with others.

We seem to have created this culture whereby to say how good you are at something is perceived as bragging and arrogant. Isn't that crazy? We need to encourage ourselves and others to be fully aware of our strengths and be proud and happy to share them. What the world needs is for us all to be the best we can be. Go on. Shout them out from the rooftops. Work on them. Make them even more of a strength.

There is a lovely story about the incredible Irish rugby player Brian O'Driscoll (or BOD, as he is known). He was quite superb but he did go through a fallow patch: things did not quite flow, and he lacked his usual spark. But then, with a change of coach, he was back to his best and most devastating. When interviewed and asked why, his response was telling (and I paraphrase): 'Under the old coach I was trying to improve in areas I was not good at, but, under the new coach, he is just asking me to shine at what I am good at.' Enough said.

Weaknesses

Well, yes, I suppose. I know what I am not so good at, and it links very closely to what does not excite me. So we can put the two together. Clearly if I am working in a space where my skills do not match what is required I will not add great value, and nor will I be enjoying myself – the idea of a square peg in a round hole comes to mind. So let's grow our understanding of the things we are not good at, or those that don't excite us, and let's try either to avoid doing them or create a team around us with the skills to complement.

As leaders, we must help the people in our team to work in an environment where their skills match the post; it is our responsibility. And, as individuals, we must endeavour to do the same for ourselves. One of the major reasons for poor performance is a lack of alignment between the capability and the role – and I am pretty sure where the responsibility for that lies: with both the person and the leader.

Limits

Really? Do you know your limits? How do you know? Have you tested them? Limits tend to create the concept of limiting beliefs, in that we cannot actually prove them. Limiting beliefs hold us back. To say, 'Oh, I can't dance' means you will never try. I did not know I could skipper a yacht around the world until I tried it. I did not know I could ski 360 miles to the Magnetic North Pole (and win) until I tried it. I know how many press-ups might be my limit today, but not tomorrow (with a bit of training). The admission 'Oh, I couldn't run a marathon' is not true. My very good friend Chris Moon has run a number of ultra-marathons, and he has only one arm and one leg!

Limits are measured in time and are perceptions or beliefs and not a known reality. That said, of course there will be some physical limits for each of us just through some basic mechanics (I doubt I would be a very great high jumper), but, and here is the crux, if we focus our activity on our strengths and on what we enjoy, then who actually knows our limits? Sober, I might say, 'I can't dance.' A couple of light ales later and it's a case of 'John Travolta, eat your heart out!' It's about limiting beliefs.

Motivations

What lights our fire? What turns us on? What is important to us? This is the bit beneath the surface that drives our behaviours. This is key to understanding the two above. The only way to fully understand your motivations is to reflect and discover them in an environment where you are not influenced by external strong cultures or other people.

I will talk more about ways to discover your inner motivations later as we discuss understanding what drives you and others and how to tap into those motivations to gain commitment. But, yes, we do need to understand deeply what actually motivates us.

Goals

Where are you heading in life? It's funny, really, but we would never dream of not setting a target for a business or a sporting team, or even an intention for a holiday, but for some reason we don't 'goal' ourselves so readily. There is a lovely Chinese saying that roughly translates as, 'Worry not about moving slowly, fear standing still.' In other words, if you are heading towards some target or goal and making progress, even if it is slow, then all is well. Discontentment can come from drifting, feeling lost or that nagging doubt that you are not going anywhere. Give yourself targets, near and far, and write them down, share them, and go for them, then you might just get there. This also links into our thinking on motivation – motivation towards a goal. A word of warning here, there is a strong Buddhist belief that setting goals negatively impacts the ability to be present. There is also great danger in setting goals that are not actually your own, but are derived through being influenced by others and by dominant cultures. But by being true to yourself, being present in the moment and having the courage to follow your own life's path you will be able to set goals that fulfil your real self-worth, and all will be well.

Needs

Sometimes these words repeat or overlap. What is the difference between needs and motivations or beliefs? It matters not. The important thing here is that people relate to their own words. If *needs* is clearer to you than *motivations*, then great. What do I need? I need loving, a challenge, to feel I am moving forward, friends, exercise, lots of different stimuli. All these needs tell me and others more about who Manley Hopkinson really is. What are your needs? Write them down.

Beliefs

These are deep-seated, less likely to change in life, potentially hard to share or for others to see. They are the core of who you are. When we consider our beliefs we generally look at our religious convictions and our intransigent thinking. These beliefs can lend themselves to acting towards an aspiration. I am firmly of the belief that we are guardians of this planet and not its owners, and that, as we are capable of conscious thought, we should act for the benefit of all sentient beings. This planet is not here for our disposal. It is all we have. This one belief drives a number of behaviours around killing or not killing, destroying or not destroying. (I use only environmentally friendly cleaning products. My toothbrush is made from bamboo (and natural bristles). Microbeads are the devil's dandruff ... What are *your* beliefs?)

Values

We discuss what values are in Chapter 9. There are some standard 'value' words that we can use. I often hear *honesty, integrity* and *empathy*, but my concern with these words is that they can mean too much and too little. When you're considering your own values, the words you would use that describe you and influence your actions, don't worry if it is perceived as a 'value' word. Just consider what it means to you. I also consider values to have an aspirational element. I may use some to describe who I am now, but I can use others to help me act in a certain way: when I cite 'courage' as one of my values, I do not always live up to it; I strive to be courageous, but I am fallible. Consider your own 'now' values and add a few 'aspirational' ones.

Priorities

These change in life – and even in a day – but they have a massive impact on your behaviour. They can be easy to share and easy for others to spot: It's getting close to lunchtime, so I'm hungry. A few years ago I did not have children; now I do. As a young man with no responsibilities and cares I was free to act and say yes to any opportunity; now, I have a family to support (and I love it) and must consider my responsibilities (priorities) before I charge ahead. As an executive coach, I prioritise listening with the intention of understanding. As a junior rugby coach, I prioritise the overall development of the children and not fulfilling my own desire for success. List your priorities of today, but review them frequently, as they will change.

Presumptions

I have a presumption in that I sincerely believe that everyone means well. This leads to my tending to trust first, to assume that your intentions are positive and compassionate. Even though I have been stung by this presumption, I maintain it. It makes me feel that all is well, or can be well, with the world if our intentions are pure. It is easy to presume that our message has been understood. The word *presumptions* could be interchanged with *beliefs* in this context, but the 'badge' in itself is irrelevant – it is what it means to you that counts.

Presumption can lead to tension. I hear people say when defining who they are that they 'don't suffer fools gladly'. Well, who are we to presume anyone else is a fool? We can 'presume' that another's goals and motivations are the same as ours and carry on, blissfully unaware that they are pulling in a different direction and are excited by completely different things. I may enjoy beer and rugby, but do you? Dare I *presume* that you do too?

Prejudices

These are the filters we put in place that get in the way or influence us. We all have prejudices, most of which are completely unfounded. I am frequently asked to talk at schools at the end of the year, to motivate and hand out the awards. At one school, as the kids were coming into the auditorium, I found myself making instant character assessments: 'Yup, academic sitting at the front. That one looks sporty. Bit of a geek there.' And with each phrase I felt closer to them or further apart: some I could relate to as I externalised my own motivations and character; others I felt I had little in common with. Then two goths came in, a boy and a girl, and went to sit in the top left-hand corner. I instantly dismissed them and, even as I scanned the room during my presentation, I found myself missing out that top left corner. And so I gave my talk, I presented the awards and shook the hands of those who came forth, received the applause and, as they streamed out into a new world, I started to pack my things. 'Excuse me, Manley. That was superb. Thank you.' I turned round and there, the first of the students to come and say thank you, speaking in an educated accent, hands outstretched to shake mine, were the two goths! Outwardly I smiled and we spoke of their dreams and aspirations, and I saw in them much of what I saw in myself as a young man. Internally, I was hugely embarrassed and cross with myself: Who the hell do you think you are, Manley, you arrogant fool? How dare you prejudge and dismiss? Never, never again!

It is within us all to be prejudiced, and it is within us all to be *aware* of our prejudices. And this is potentially one of the biggest blockers to the whole principle of Compassionate Leadership. Go on, be honest: what are *your* prejudices?

Experiences

When we look back at our lives and remember what experiences we have had, we ought not merely to reflect in the activity but consider what we've learned along the way. Be aware of how the memory makes you feel. What emotion does it solicit in you? Have you put on those rose-coloured spectacles in your reflection? (I know I do, and I am not always best served by that.) I find it amusing to share a joint experience with someone and realise how differently we both look at the same experience. There is a lovely expression: 'The child is the father of the man.' It means all that has gone on before makes us who we are now. I think this exercise will, and should, take some time. Don't rush it, be present and enjoy the process. It will make you smile and, at times, possibly cry. All of us have a story inside us. What was your journey so far? What is your story? What is your song?

Behaviours

I reckon this one is tough to nail down. How do I behave? How do you behave? How do you know? All the other stuff above informs how we behave. What words would you use? And in this case try to be real and not aspirational. I find that passing these by people who really know you can be a real eye opener! In fact, as we develop our 'knowing me', it is what others think that has more power. Write down how you think you behave. Aristotle said, 'We are what we repeatedly do; excellence therefore, is not an act, but a habit.' Wise man! To act in a particular way once does not define you, but to do something repeatedly becomes a visible behaviour and affects how others define you.

Character

I reckon I could be described as an outgoing, gregarious, optimistic, trusting, fun, energetic, easygoing kind of chap. But my wife might put down some other words, like frustrating, irresponsible, loud. And this is the beauty of the whole principle of Me, You and Us: the more we can raise our 'knowing me', the less will be the difference between what we say, what we do and who we are – and that, my friend, is the secret!

How we are perceived by others

This is it! This is the one! Understanding the way we are perceived by others is vital to becoming a Compassionate Leader. If we can understand how we are being perceived by others, then, and only then, do we have a chance to modify our behaviour to suit the situation. If we blissfully and blindly stumble on, just doing our thing and being totally impervious to the impact of our actions on others, we will not become that Compassionate Leader. Our relationships will struggle and we will become confused as our intent does not match the reaction. The chances of creating a 'committed' team around us are slim. When you reflected on your behaviour and character, you observed from your own station. Now try to step outside yourself and observe you from afar. Then, having done that, share your findings with the ones who know you most or with the ones you are trying to influence. There are many '360-degree' surveys we can do. I urge you to do as many as you can, but, better than that, just ask people for feedback as regularly as you can.

Emotions

It appears that, in a male-dominated, corporate, Western society, we struggle with the concept of emotions. It is almost as if it is a weakness to have any. What rot! They are within us all at all times and have the largest impact on how we behave. To deny our emotions is to deny ourselves. It is to ignore our motivations and our needs. There is a reason why emotional intelligence is so-called: it is the area of life where we can develop the most, where we can make the biggest gains and where we can make the biggest impact. This time it is not about listing our emotions, as all emotions are within us all – anger, sadness, despair, hope, love. The key is understanding what is *driving* our emotions. And which emotions are to the fore at a specific moment.

My anger stems from a different source from yours, as does my happiness, but, if I know which emotion is to the fore at any moment, then, instead of reacting to that emotion in an unconscious and instinctive way, I have a chance to control it, rationalise it, enjoy it – but never to deny it or suppress it – and then, and only then, can I consciously choose the behaviour that is best suited to the situation.

We need to understand our emotions and what is happening within us. The key thing here is that, if we understand our emotions, we can decide whether or not to modify our behaviour. I'm sure there are times in all of our lives when we've said something and wished we hadn't, when we've reacted in a particular way, an emotional way, and it didn't have the impact we wanted. Once we understand what's happening internally, that has a massive impact on what we do externally. By 'knowing me'.

So, now you know the areas in which you need to raise your self-awareness, you need to do it.

But how? How are you going to develop your self-awareness

and grow your 'me-aware'? There are two exercises I would like you to do now: the 'Me Aware' and the 'Iceberg'.

EXERCISE: ME AWARE

Spend some time in quiet reflection. Listen to the opinions of others. Seek feedback on yourself.

Gather all the information you can on yourself, then write down your strengths, weaknesses, limits, motivations, goals, needs, beliefs, values, priorities, presumptions, prejudices, experiences, behaviours, character – and other variations on the themes.

Include the critical headings of: 'How we are perceived by others' and 'Our emotions'.

You can make your own headings here of course. Who am I to direct your thinking? Frequently, I ask groups, 'What is it you need to know about yourself?' And then work with what they create.

Use the grid examples to help you.

Me aware	Remarks
Strengths	Really good at understanding the big picture.
	I can motivate a team to gain commitment.
Weaknesses	Tend to gloss over the details.
	Sometimes it would be better if I did more research.
	Sometimes jump to conclusions – should listen better.
Prejudices	I struggle with people I think are arrogant or look down on me or others.
Emotions	Generally under control, though I do have a tendency to get cross or irritated when I see … What makes me happy is … What makes me sad is …
How others perceive me	I think, friendly, enthusiastic, confident.
	But it could be loud, arrogant.

EXERCISE: THE ICEBERG

Here we use the metaphor of an iceberg to help frame this idea and articulate our thinking.

This is an exercise in visualisation. You may well know that, due to the relative densities of ice and water, only about one-ninth of an iceberg is above the surface. This is a great way to look at ourselves and think of the visible berg as representing our visible self – our behaviours – and the eight-ninths beneath the water as all the factors that influence who we are.

There are a number of levels we need to consider.

Nature

Deep at the base of the berg we have our nature – what is 'hard-wired' within. There is so much about us that 'just is'. It is the way you look at the world, make decisions and plan yourself, as well as your more physical attributes. Within your leadership career you may have carried out various personality assessments such as the Myers–Briggs type indicator or the Strength Deployment Inventory (a suite of psychometric tests) – and there are many more. These are all great and add to the jigsaw puzzle that is ourselves. None of them is a complete assessment. Rather, they help to complete the picture.

For example, if I were to do my own 'Iceberg' exercise, I would be forced to share at the very bottom of my iceberg that I am, well, some would say disorganised. But that is not exactly fair. I know I need deadlines. If I have three months to complete a task, I will work on big-picture stuff for two and a half months, then work late and long in the final couple of weeks to complete. If I am packing for a holiday, it all happens the morning of departure. My wife, on the other hand, would plan slightly more and think ahead. These things are hard-wired and make up the 'nature' element of who we are.

→

Nurture and life experiences

The middle part is made up of all the life experiences, the early nurturing parts below and a choreography of events, all of which have fashioned who we are. So many specific experiences would have impacted on your more adult life. For example, my father was in the Royal Navy, so we moved house every two and a half years. This has had the effect that I come from 'nowhere' and struggle to settle; I am always looking 'over the fence' just to check if it might be greener.

A 'nurturing' event would have been that time when my mother told me off (see Chapter 1). Boy, what an impact!

As we come up the iceberg, closer to the surface, what lies in the depths impacts on us and fashions our motivations, values and beliefs. You can use the output from the 'Big Journey' exercise here (see p. 70), but really reflect hard on which words to use to describe your motivations, values and beliefs – it is the most important part.

Our filters

These are our assumptions, preconceptions and priorities. Just before what we've discussed so far comes to the surface to see the light of day and be visible to others as our behaviour, we apply our filters.

I spoke before about how our preconceived ideas can lead to prejudices and disable us from relating to others – for instance, my goth story (shameful, sorry!).

My filters might include: always being optimistic, wearing 'rose tinted spectacles' and some negative ones too like, 'not too good at listening sometimes' ...

So capture your 'filters' just below the surface.

External factors – the 'weather'

One other aspect to consider will be the external factors (or 'weather') that impact on how you behave at the moment.   ➡

These are outside of ourselves and potentially out of our control, too. It could be that you are in the middle of moving house, or a merger or acquisition, or your teenage daughter has just gone off to university.

Now we come up from our deep dive and reflect on how we actually behave. I think this is the toughest part, but give it your best shot. Reflect on what you have already captured at various depths of your iceberg, and remember not to be aspirational here, but to be as objective as you possibly can be.

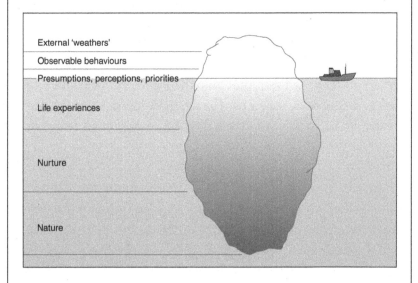

External 'weathers'

Observable behaviours

Presumptions, perceptions, priorities

Life experiences

Nurture

Nature

Figure 5.3 Our iceberg, and what lurks below the surface

So there you have it! Your iceberg – an ice sculpture of your inner self.

This exercise is best done on a big sheet of paper, and mapped onto the image of an iceberg – it makes it all the more memorable and easier to share (remember UMU).

Work on your iceberg over time, refine it, enjoy it, share it.

Knowing you

So, if we need to know all that stuff about ourselves, then what do we need to know about others?

Facilitating this question is always amusing, as people start to look at the list about 'Knowing Me', ticking them off one by one. Then it dawns on them: 'I need to know exactly the same about others as I do about myself.' The same characteristics, the needs, motivations and all!

We do indeed need to know the same about other people as we know about ourselves. We need to know our motivations, our intentions, how we're perceived, our values, beliefs, emotions. Likewise, we need to know the same about the people we're with. Simple!

But how? People will not always share of themselves. If I struggle to know me, how am I going to know you? This is a key concept: *it is through our self-awareness that we develop an empathy for others.*

If I have a desire to know me, it will create the desire to know you. If I am ignorant of me, what is to drive my wish to know you? How can I motivate you if I do not know what motivates you? Invariably, I will externalise my own motivations and impose those on you.

Consider this scenario. You are driving along in a bit of traffic and you notice in your rear-view mirror an ambulance, blue lights flashing, trying to weave its way through the traffic. What do you do? Of course, you move over. Now, a few moments later you see a ubiquitous 'white van' trying to muscle its way through. Now what do you do? When I ask this question the normal response is, 'Slow them down', 'Give them the finger' and other such expressions of frustration and anger. However, what if you knew that the child of the driver of the white van was in that ambulance? Now what would you do? Of course, now you would let them go.

This is the difference. You knew the motivation of the ambulance. You did not know the motivation of the white-van driver. You just externalised your own motivations or frustrations with an 'If *I* can't get through why should they?' mentality. On reflection, you know that is irrational and may indeed be very, very wrong. This actually happened to a friend, and the effort he had to put in to follow the ambulance was extraordinary and reflected the effort people put in to try to stop him. If only they'd known his predicament and motivation, then ...

If we react only to a behaviour we might be getting the wrong end of the stick and making matters worse. If I can develop 'knowing you', I have chance to respond with the right behaviour and judge you on your motivation and needs and not on mine! If I know your motivations, I can understand your behaviour.

As a leader, how can I compliment or encourage individuals in my team if I do not know what they value and where they derive self-worth? If I compliment them based on *my* idea of what *I* need, it will not be a compliment. If I recognise them based on *my* desire for recognition, they will not see it.

EXERCISE: YOU AWARE

Carry out the Me Aware exercise from p. 61 with a person you are trying to build a relationship with – or maybe one you are struggling to create a good relationship with (I've used the example of Mike in the table below). Depending on the depth of your relationship, this can be done by making informed guesses as to what their answers might be.

Or, you could sit down and open conversation – they ought to know themselves better than you do!   ⟶

Mike	My perception/agreed perception
Strengths	Good at planning.
	Good financial and business brain.
Weaknesses	Doesn't understand the 'human' or emotional side of life.
	Not good at listening.
Prejudices	I think he considers emotions to be soft.
Etc. ...	(Time to be honest again.)
Emotions	Haven't spotted any apart from frustration.
How do I perceive him?	Cold, unemotional.

Wow! Clearly there is a disconnect here. So what am I going to do about it?

When you discover a disconnect you have two options: you can blame the other person or look at what you can do. As with any difference, you can make it a barrier or an opportunity to resolve differences and move forward.

Think for a few moments about how you would handle it.

This exercise is superb at highlighting relationship issues and at pinpointing the major perception differences that cause the tension. What you do about the revelations is up to you.

Johari's Window

A good model to look at to position the importance of 'knowing me' and 'knowing you' is Johari's Window. I like this model for a number of reasons: it is closely aligned to my UMU principle in that I can draw it, explain it, understand it and use it on a daily basis. And I like the humour: the name Johari sounds like some Middle Eastern thinker sitting atop a large hill and with big ear lobes. However, it was instead created by two Americans, Jo and Hari (Joseph Luft and Harrington Ingham)!

Johari's Window explores what we know about ourselves and each other, and what we can use to build in a relationship.

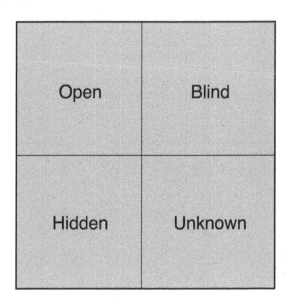

Figure 5.4 Johari's Window – closed

Whatever is in the open space in the window we can use. What's hidden, blind or unknown, we cannot. The hidden and blind limit our ability to relate to the other. Our blind and unknown limit our own abilities. It is only in the open space that we can operate effectively together.

Through feedback, you help me reduce my blind; through sharing, I put more in the open space to use; and, through either self-discovery or observation linked with sharing and feedback, I reduce the size of my self-limiting unknown. We will, of course, share only so much, or give so much feedback. I need to know that whatever I put on the table or in the open window you will use to best intent.

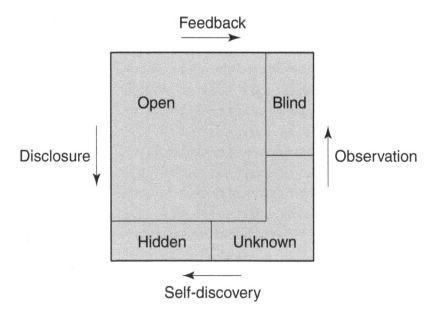

Figure 5.5 Johari's Window – opened!

And this leads into the 'us' space of our Me, You and Us model and, once again, back to the concept of Compassionate Leadership. So:

- by raising my 'knowing you' I have the chance of responding to your motivation and not judging your behaviour
- raising my 'knowing you' allows me to behave to achieve the best outcome in any situation
- by raising my 'knowing you' I can match your activity to your needs, likes and skills
- by raising my 'knowing you' I can tap into your motivations and needs and help fulfil your self-esteem
- by raising my 'knowing you' I can gain your commitment over your compliance
- by raising my 'knowing you' I am another step closer to being a Compassionate Leader

And it makes me feel good too!

EXERCISE: THE BIG JOURNEY

This exercise can be done individually and is powerful in helping us find our 'true self'. It is also extremely powerful in a team environment, as it taps into all three elements of the Me, You and Us model.

You can use this exercise right now, and I would recommend that you do so before taking it into your teams. You will then have an authentic understanding of the exercise and be better able to facilitate it with your team.

Or, preferably, you could drop me a line and I will come and work it through with you – with all my splendid pictures, videos and stories!

For this exercise you will need:

- your imagination

- three sticky notes (for the team exercise, or any writing pad if just for you alone)

- a pen or pencil

- a bit of quiet time: about 30 minutes for you, and an hour or so with the team

This story is one of my 'Inspiring Talks' and core to my work on cultural transformations – www.manleytalks.com.

Picture the scene. You are about to take part in the BT Global Challenge, the World's toughest yacht race – 32,000 miles and 9 months of a life-changing odyssey.

There will be 12 identical 72-foot, 40-ton steel yachts that will battle for honours in this incredible race. The boats are equal down to the last number of knives, forks, winch handles and sails. So this race is not about best boat or biggest budget: it is about the crew – and you are one of them!

So with whom are you sailing? You are one of 27 crew ➡

volunteers from all walks of life and from all over the world. Eight of you have never sailed before committing to take on this incredible adventure. The youngest is 21 and the eldest 62. There is a 'core crew' of 15 who will sail all the way round the world – and you are one of them. Then the other 12 take it in turns to join the boat, two at a time, for just one leg of the race – they are called the 'leggers'.

This team will need to be strong, because you are about to race around the world, the 'wrong way'! By that I mean 'west about'. Leaving Southampton in the UK, you will battle your way across the North Atlantic against the prevailing winds and against the mighty Gulf Stream – that massive body of water that marches across the Atlantic bringing with it anything float-ing within. If the wind is strong, it will punch you on the nose, and, if the wind is light, the Gulf Stream will drag you back whence you came.

From Boston, and after only a couple of weeks' respite to rebuild your energies and repair the boat, you will head south, through the Hurricane Belt in hurricane season, across the Doldrums, that vast swathe of mid-world ocean with light and fickle winds and hot humid conditions. Then it's down the coast of South America before you battle your way up the muddy waters of the River Plate to arrive in Buenos Aeries some 5,800 miles later.

Now the crews are becoming tense, as the next leg of over 6,000 nautical miles takes you around the dreaded Cape Horn at the tip of South America and past Tierra del Fuego – the Land of Fire – before you have to crash your way across the mighty Southern Ocean. At times you will be over 1,800 miles away from land, just you and your crewmates pushing the boat hard in freezing, storm-bound conditions. You arrive in Wellington to a hero's welcome: not many folk hit the coast of New Zealand from the east, and the Kiwis respect any who do – and you will be a pretty special crew by then.   ⟶

Here the boats come out of the water, the masts are taken down and a three-week refit takes place. You venture into the beautiful landscapes of New Zealand – the land of the long white cloud – to take stock of your journey, regroup and refocus before you take on the Southern Ocean for the second time.

But, before heading for the deep south, you make your way across the Tasman Sea to Sydney. Only one week long, that leg is no less draining, as all the teams are pushing the boats hard and many have VIP guests on board – they need to impress.

After you leave behind the delights of Sydney, it does not take long for the oceans to force a reckoning as a storm strikes the fleet in the notorious Bass Straits. One boat is damaged with injured crew and must return to Australia. The rest of the fleet wish them well but sail on, deeper and deeper south, knowing what lies ahead this time. The storms keep rolling in, one after the other, with barely time to catch your breath in between. As you crest the peaks of the mighty Southern Ocean rollers, the wind accelerates, screaming in the rigging. Falling off the crest, you roll back down to the relative calm of the wave trough, craning your neck as you look up at the next breaking crest coming your way. The wind tricks you as you come up to Cape Town, leaving you becalmed – meaning motionless, lacking wind – in a fog bank only a few miles offshore. As the fog clears, you see the mighty Cape and creep in, arriving to massive party scenes well after midnight.

The worst is over, as from Cape Town there are only two legs of the race left. The long difficult leg north crosses the Equator for a second time, where, as tradition decrees, an offering is made to Neptune, with the inexperienced crew made to suffer! (To put your mind at rest, the offering tends to be in the form of leftover food (slops) which is also thrown over the 'first timers' to make them suffer!)

The fun over, the Doldrums creep up on you. This is when you realise that having not enough wind is more exhausting ➡

than having too much, as you battle to reach every little zephyr that touches the sea to gain some momentum and leave this sticky, tricky hell. You pass through, only for Madeira to tease you, but, eventually, after almost 40 days at sea, you sense the welcoming sensations that reach out to you in the Bay of Biscay as the good food, plentiful wine and a sailors' welcome that only the French can do awaits you in beautiful La Rochelle.

A few short days later, the final test is upon you as, only four days on, the most intense sailing of your life separates you from your loved ones and a homecoming that will stay with you for the rest of your days. Four days of no sleep, constant sail changes and a close fleet. You round the bottom of the Isle of Wight, sailing deep into Poole Bay, before charging through the narrows at Hurst Castle into a Solent packed with boats of all sizes to see you in.

Then it is all over.

You cross the line. Pack away the sails for the very last time. You stop as you do so and keep your hand on the yacht. 'Thank you,' you whisper to her for seeing you safely home.

The biggest party ever – and you are home!

So let me take you back.

This is the first time we have met and the first time you have met your team. You are about to embark on this incredible race, but, before you do, I have three questions to ask.

On your first sticky note, I want you to write your name – own everything you do. Then write down your answer to this: 'What is in this for me?' In other words, what is your selfish takeaway? What is it you want just for yourself from taking part in the BT Global Challenge? Go on, write your thoughts now.

On the second note, I want you to capture the look and feel of the team. Which words would you like others to use when describing you as a team in the BT Global Challenge?

On the third note, capture what you want to achieve for the race.

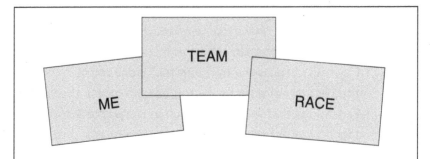

Figure 5.6 Stick it on the sticky notes

If you are doing this exercise with your team, ask them to share with their neighbour for a few minutes, then capture the words on three big flipcharts.

Having done this, announce that you are going to disappoint them, as I am you now – hopefully for the first and last time!

For you are no longer sailing around the world. You are you, doing whatever it is you normally do – you are back at work, and life is as it was.

Now look at your 'me' notes. Which ones are now no longer relevant? Any? I bet none. Of course.

Go to the words you wrote on the second note, about the 'look and feel' of the team. Do you want to change any of those? Nope?

Isn't it brilliant! You see, it does not matter what we are actually doing, for what you wrote down is what you want. The first is what you want for yourself – to learn, feel a sense of pride, accomplishment, to be challenged, get out of your comfort zone, to achieve, to make friends, to have fun, even see the world. Of course you still want that. That is the beauty!

And the second note describes how you want the team to be, in other words how you want your work environment to be. You want it to be disciplined, determined, focused, organised, fun, supportive, successful, honest and open – of course you do!

And the third note gives you a glimpse of your core motivations, which we will discuss later in the book! ➡️

This exercise is so incredibly powerful. By using metaphor in a reflective way, you can be true to your inner self without being influenced by your peers or the dominant culture of your workplace – like the eight-year-old you we spoke about in Chapter 5 (see Fig 5.2 on p. 49), you are able to respond in ways that are true to yourself, your own character and value set. When you share this true inner self with your colleagues it has a massive impact on your Johari's Window (p. 69) and helps you to take a major step towards creating meaningful relationships with your colleagues.

The revelations through this exercise also:

- form the core of my work in creating commitment through cultural alignment, which we will explore further in Chapter 9, and

- create the first steps of true ownership in whole organisational cultural transformation!

It's amazing that all this can come from three sticky notes, a story and half an hour of your time!

I love this exercise. It is so brilliantly simple yet such an eye opener!

Knowing us

And so we reach the third part of our Me, You and Us model. What does that mean?

The 'us' is the environment we create that allows us to share, to give and receive feedback, to realise we're here to get the best out of each other and to grow together in many respects.

The 'us' is the environment associated with Compassionate Leadership. You will not share anything if you do not trust what I might do with it. Why would you let me know how you feel, or what your weaknesses might be, if I am to bash you over the head with it? Here's a behavioural example where your best intentions could be misinterpreted: do you coach a strength or a weakness? If you are good at something and I help you excel in it, how will that make you feel? Consider that reinforcement of self-worth through self-esteem and self-respect. However, if I focused on your weaknesses, on what you are not good at, which also tends to correlate with what you do not enjoy, how will that make you feel? My intention was to help you and improve your ability to add value. The result could well be the opposite.

Remember that quote from the Dalai Lama I shared at the beginning of the book? 'Empathy is a desire to know the other person. Compassion is to act on that knowledge with positive intent.'

Me, You and Us develops trust in a relationship, and that is the foundation of all relationships. Me, You and Us is a real UMU model: it helps us **understand** emotional intelligence; we can **memorise** it through the stories and the exercises we can do; and we can **use** it in all life situations – immediately.

This creates a real, strong and deep understanding of self, similar understanding about the other person, and creating a safe environment that allows you to share and grow together.

We can apply this concept in every area of our lives. When we look at leadership, at power and influence, we can apply Me, You and Us. What is it that we know about ourselves and others that would give hints to our power bases and means of influence?

When we're thinking about how to develop people, clearly we need to know about Me, You and Us. In all aspects of relationships – at home, at work, at leisure – the key understanding of self is the beginning of it all. In many respects, leadership is like 'inside out': relationship starts inside, then you can go outside with the leadership.

To me, this chapter is the summary of the attitude of mature and emotionally intelligent Compassionate Leadership. I have witnessed the concept of Me, You and Us woven into every element of leadership and relationships. Without the opportunity to discover what you know about yourself and others, and without the tools to create the environment that allows both to grow, success is limited at best.

In essence, it is about balance.

Just before I leave a chapter that is about knowing you, me and us, I'd like to add something that's a pet hate: simple words, but they can create a damaging attitude.

People vs resources

We often hear in the rooms and corridors of corporate life that people lack 'resources'. 'I need more resources.' 'OK, we can ditch those resources.' 'Can I relocate some of your resources?' And here I'm referring specifically to the way the word *resources* is used as a synonym for *people*, not within its wider meaning of materials and equipment.

I hate it. It conveniently takes away the emotional fact that you are dealing with people. Real people, with emotional needs. I'm not just a 'resource'! A table is a resource. So is a book, a computer, money and a million other inanimate objects that we need to do our work. I'm a human being. I'm awkward, costly, confusing. I have emotional needs, damn it!

Calling me an 'FTE' (full-time employee) is even worse. But at least the *E* bit implies a touch of humanity.

You are a leader. A Compassionate Leader. You want to create a committed, long-lasting, high-performing, overachieving group of individuals, people, who, collectively, will change the world, will deliver, and deliver again and again, all the time looking for ways to be better, to do it better, to grow, learn and improve. Imagine that. You don't need 'resources': you need people!

And this is why, when I join the senior leadership team of any company, I take on the title of 'People and Performance' – because that's what it is all about!

Key Learnings

The foundation of emotional intelligence is Me, You and Us:

- fostering the desire to know more about 'me'.

- striving to understand 'you'.

- creating the constructive environment that allows 'us' to grow and develop.

When we look at what we need to influence people, it's all about the universal goal of self-worth.

Understanding your own emotions is key to your success as a leader.

The Johari Window explores what we know about each other and what we can build in a relationship. Whatever is in the 'open' space in the window, we can use to develop a relationship. What is hidden, blind or unknown, we cannot.

People are not mere resources. People are people, too.

EXERCISE: ME CIRCLE

When you have carried out the 'Big Journey' exercise, complete a 'me circle' by listing all the facets about yourself that you know.

When you've done that, revisit the 'Iceberg' exercise you did earlier. What is hard-wired about you? Which early-life experiences can you remember as a key part of your nurturing? Your meaningful life experiences? Your motivations, values and beliefs? What filters do you apply? What 'external weather' is also affecting your behaviour? And, finally, can you write down your behaviour?

Notes

_____

_____

_____

_____

_____

_____

_____

_____

_____

_____

_____

_____

_____

_____

CHAPTER 6

WHAT LIGHTS MY FIRE?

Why does anyone do what they do? Why do I want to make this next step? Why do I want to change my behaviour? Why should I do it this way and not the way I've been doing it for many years? Why should I do want you want? Or why should *you* do what *I* want?

As we discussed in the previous chapter, if you break down the response to any act or change it comes down to 'self-benefit' ('self-interest' or 'self-worth') – I do this or that because it benefits me.

Here's a lovely story that has been passed down from generation to generation, about self-interest that I'd like to share with you.

The Farmer and the Apple Tree That Stopped Bearing Fruit

A farmer had an apple tree that had stopped bearing fruit (as the title suggests). 'Ah, shame!' sighed the farmer. 'This apple tree doesn't bear me any fruit and has no use to me, so I'll chop it down.' Moments later he returned with a sharp axe. As his axe cut into the tree, he disturbed a bird and a cricket that had both made their home in the old apple tree. Alarmed, the bird and the cricket spoke in chorus: 'Farmer, what are ⟶

you doing? Why are you chopping the tree down? This is our home.'

The farmer explained that the tree no longer bore any fruit and that it was of no use to him, so he was chopping it down for firewood. The bird and the cricket explained, 'But it has use to us. It's where we live. Please don't chop it down.'

The farmer replied, 'No, I'm sorry. It has no use to me. It has to go.'

The bird and the cricket promised to sing and chirp and make it a beautiful environment for the farmer, so he'd want to sit under the tree and relax. But the farmer replied with, 'No, sorry, cricket and bird, but that still doesn't help me. I'm chopping it down.'

As he started chopping the tree down, he cut through to the centre and disturbed a bees' nest. Honey started oozing out of the tree.

The farmer said to himself, Honey! I love honey! This tree is now sacred.

From that moment on the farmer always preserved the tree!

This Aesop fable is one of self-interest. There is self-interest in preservation of the tree now because the farmer has use for it, due to his liking for honey.

In everything we do, we must understand that we need to sell self-interest to ourselves and also to the people we're trying to influence.

The big sell is to realise the self-worth in everything we do. You've read about the need and the benefits in gaining commitment as opposed to forcing compliance. To gain the commitment of other people to your course of action demands that you be able to sell the self-benefit of that action to them.

Why should I empower my people? Why should I get them

to be committed instead of compliant? I'm too busy to waste time coaching or explaining; just do it! Compliance may work in the short term, but, if I make a *committed* team, I'll get so much more out of them, they'll do so much more, they'll stay with me longer, they'll be happier in themselves, which – no matter how you look at it, whether from an altruistic or hard-nosed, commercial perspective – sounds good and will be more productive. It means they need less supervision from me; in the longer term I'm freer to achieve more; I grow (a 'me' benefit); they grow (a 'you' benefit); we all grow (an 'us' benefit). All of these are benefits that I can sell to myself from the idea of creating a committed team instead of a compliant one, of motivating the individuals within a team and the team as a whole to achieve. So a lot of the 'sell' of a lot of the lessons of the book is 'How can I realise a benefit to myself?' 'How can I sell the benefit to the team or the other person involved?'

Three needs

Here is a superb model I have used to help understand the different motivations that I will need to address within a team if I am to succeed in selling the benefit I need.

The American psychological theorist David McClelland asserted that an individual's needs are influenced by their cultural background and life experiences. He also asserted, in his 'Three Needs Theory', that the majority of these needs can be classified as the needs for affiliation, achievement and influence. The importance of each will vary from one person to another. If you can determine that importance, it will help you decide how to influence and motivate people.

As a leader, I find it is possible to increase a person's motivation and effectiveness through an environment that provides them with their ideal mix of these three needs. This model can be accessed through a self-assessment. It is easy to use and it gives you not only a better understanding of your own motivations, but also an insight into reading the motivational needs of others. If your team has this understanding in advance of the rough seas, think of the advantage it will give you when you're in the eye of the storm.

I have used this theory to great effect on many occasions, and one particular example comes to mind.

I mentioned earlier that I was fortunate enough to skipper a yacht in the BT Global Challenge. As you may recall from Chapter 5, there were 12 identical 72-foot, 40-ton steel yachts battling for honours. The boats were equal in all respects. So this race is not about best boat or biggest budget: it is about the crew – a motley bunch of 27 crew volunteers from all walks of life and from all over the world. Eight of the crew had never sailed before committing themselves to this extreme adventure. The youngest of my crew was 21 and the eldest 62. The 'core crew' of 15 sailed all the way round the world, and there were two 'leggers', who joined the boat, two at a time, for just one leg of the race. So we had a racing complement of 18 – one professional skipper (myself) and 17 amateur crew.

We were known as 'Team Large' – and I'll have more to say about that in Chapter 9.

On the second leg of the race, as we left Boston on our way to Buenos Aries, we knew there were two big obstacles in our way: the Doldrums, that band of windless, hot, humid air that spans the Equator and frustrates many a sailor as they try to pass through; and, before that, the Hurricane Belt – and we would be passing through it in the hurricane season.

We had a great start and sailed out of Boston with the sun and the wind on our backs into warming seas and beautiful skies. I am not a particularly religious man, but I am very spiritual and believe that, no matter what your religious or spiritual persuasion, in environments of great beauty and tranquillity, where we can comprehend the scale of Mother Nature, one feels closer to one's maker. I remember one particular beautiful evening sky with a fresh breeze and a following sea.

We were trucking along sweetly, competing well with most of the fleet behind. The sun was setting behind a range of clouds with streams of light pouring through like heavenly tracks tinting the clouds and the sea (when I was a kid I used to think that was God speaking to someone). All was well with our little world.

Part of my philosophy as a leader and skipper was that this was a superb opportunity for us all to learn more about ourselves, self-awareness being the first element of relationship and Compassionate Leadership. We had a saying on our yacht: 'If you listen hard enough, the sea answers all your questions.' In other words, shut up! Just shut up and listen to the world and your mind. Ask of yourself who you are and what you are – and then be still. This evening was one of those priceless reflective opportunities that we maximised.

By the next morning, all this was to change, as, behind every great beauty, there can lie great danger. Suddenly, our automatic 'Teletext' machine sprang into life. Every commercial vessel that plies the seas is equipped with such a global warning system of any hazards occurring in its sea area. I had disabled the audible alarm (not wanting to cause panic), but the screen woke and the cursor blinked expectantly:

HURRICANE MICHAEL FORECAST/ADVISORY NUMBER 26, NATIONAL WEATHER SERVICE MIAMI FLORIDA, AL10012100Z THU OCT 18TH 2000 . . .

So read the first part of the message. I was not overly concerned as we were in a pretty big area – the North Atlantic – and this may just have been advisory.

TROPICAL STORM CENTER LOCATED NEAR 35.4N 60.0W AT 27/2100Z . . .

I quickly checked the chart to see its relative position and suddenly my focus changed. This was going to impact on us. We were going to be 'friends' with Hurricane Michael! What had started as a hot day in the Sahara with a high energy cloud was spat out to sea. Then, with the perfect combination of air and sea temperature and the Coriolis effect of the earth's spin, it had become a full-blown hurricane that had tracked west across the ocean and was now tracking north towards us – good for America but bad for us!

So how big was Hurricane Michael (and, trust me, there are big hurricanes and bigger hurricanes)? I needed to know.

WINDS 55 KT WITH GUSTS TO 75 KT ...

Ouch! Seventy-five knots. That's 90 miles (140 kilometres) per hour. That is big, very big. To get a feel for a wind of this strength, in the Beaufort Scale a full-blown gale of Force 8 is only 38 m.p.h. – trees fall down, tiles are blown off the roofs of houses. With winds of that speed, what would the waves be like? I did not have to wait long for an answer:

SEA STATE WITHIN 200NM, EXTREMELY
ROUGH. WITHIN 100NM PHENOMENAL ...

'Phenomenal'! In all my years of sailing I had never seen a sea described as 'phenomenal'. Quickly, and subtly, checking the thesaurus of nautical meteorological terms, I looked up what 'phenomenal' means in this context. A 100-foot wave would not necessarily hurt if it were 200 yards apart from peak to peak, but a 'phenomenal' wave has a standing, breaking part of some 30 feet – that's millions of tons of water coming down on top of you like an express train.

Internally, I was in knots. Externally, I had to show calm. I had advised my crew that they could panic only if I panicked first, and now was not the time for panic. I was about to take my crew of amateur sailors into a huge hurricane and the last line of the signal did not fill me with joy:

ERRORS MAY BE LARGE. STOP

In other words, the forecasters did not know exactly what, where or how big Hurricane Michael was going to be.

Fear changes you. If you are afraid of something, it consumes you. It pumps adrenalin through your body, the blood leaves your brain and streams towards your muscles ready for freeze, flight or fight. You stop thinking rationally. You go into self-protection mode. You are in 'conflict'. If you play a game of sport carrying an injury, you will hurt yourself more, because you are focusing on that injury. If you parachute into an empty field with a single tree, you will hit the tree, because it becomes your focus. I did not want my crew to be afraid of Hurricane Michael. I had to set not only my attitude, but that of all of my crew.

I checked my thinking and I checked the facts. I called a crew meeting. I explained about the signal received. I explained about the likely track of Hurricane Michael and I explained about the implication. I said: 'Hurricane Michael is large.' There was silence.

'Wait, listen. Hurricane Michael is large, *we* are large – there is a marriage.'

Silence with a few nervous giggles and paling faces.

'Michael is large, we are large. The other yachts are running away from Hurricane Michael like frightened rabbits. We are going to attack Hurricane Michael.'

Ashen faces, bemused silence.

'We are going to attack Hurricane Michael. This is the plan. The wind is on our beam. We will always keep the wind on our beam and track into Hurricane Michael in a gentle arc. If we are disciplined with our attack, the wind will bring us into the side of the hurricane, not in front; it will not run over us. As we come in on the side and when the barometer drops at a certain rate we'll know we're so far from the eye. We'll tack out. It will zoom past us, give us a kick up the pants, and we'll come out in first place. What do you think, team?'

Those crew members whose highest motivational need was a need to achieve leapt on board with the plan straight away. 'Yeah, come on, let's attack the hurricane!' So the more 'alpha' of my team were with me.

But I had to secure the commitment from everybody in my crew. So next I needed to address those whose higher need was affiliation, belonging to a team and having a strong sense of being together, so I changed my language. I spoke about how 'Team Large', as we were known, were different from the other teams, how we were the strongest team, the only team with an identity outside the sponsor's. I talked of how we'd achieved so much before, and how we would, together, achieve so much more. This was our opportunity to show ourselves, our friends and families and the rest of the fleet just how strong Team Large were. The 'affiliators', sensing an opportunity to be a part of an even stronger team, were now on board too.

Now two-thirds of the team were behind me. But one-third of the team were still unsure, and they were the people who needed to know what was happening, needing the understanding, and, on McClelland's model, those needing to 'influence'. One of this group, shaking, white with fear, prodded me in the chest and said, 'Don't you play with my bloody life!' He and the others of this group just needed to know that they had some skin in the game, if you like.

'Right, come with me, let me explain everything I can about a hurricane.'

I asked them to repeat the 'decision factors' back to me. 'Do you understand the why and how? Yes?'

'OK, it's your call, then.' 'You decide and I will not override your decision.'

The crew member with the greatest fear was to take on the role of monitoring the barometer and would make the decision when to take us away from Hurricane Michael. It was the application of the Three Needs Theory that allowed us to attack the hurricane. That and our agreed 'culture', as defined in our 'Maximise' statement, which we'll talk about later.

Team Large was about to 'attack' the most powerful weather system on the planet, and with a total team commitment.

So how was Hurricane Michael? It was everything that hurricanes are meant to be: it really was 'large', *very* large!

It was a strange feeling heading south knowing we were about to 'attack' the hurricane. In clear blue skies and a warm wind we prepared the yacht and ourselves. Ensuring all was secure below decks, preparing storm rations (cold food that could be eaten one-handed), changing our watch system from two shifts doing four hours on and four off, to three shifts of three hours to allow the team greater rest (with fewer people on deck it is much safer too). We checked all our safety equipment, the rig and sails, and monitored the skies and instruments. Waiting. Waiting for the hit.

The first signs came with high clouds scudding across the sky. A darkness grew in the sea. The clouds thickened and blackened; the wind steadily grew. A nervous excitement gripped the crew. Some were silent, some animated, some looking around for reassurance – the Jungian traits of inner motivations were bubbling to the surface as we all got to grips with our own inner turmoil.

Hurricane Michael was all a 'large' hurricane is meant to be: wild, wicked and very, very wet. The cacophony and confusion were absolute. The seas were immense and the noise deafening. Talking and even shouting on the upper deck was a waste of time. This was the moment to test our understanding of how to sail and how to operate as a team.

There were two telling events that showed me how motivated the whole team had become with our intent to attack. The first was when we were near the heart of the storm, after we had been battling for quite a few hours. I overheard a conversation between two of my crew, neither of whom was an experienced sailor and not of the 'achievement' need.

'I reckon if we pull this rope in harder, we can go faster.' Faster! Faster! It was a beautiful moment. It was clear to me that my crew were not afraid of Hurricane Michael. What had at first appeared to be a threat was no more than an opportunity. We had successfully set the attitude. You, the leader, can choose the attitude you need and influence that of your team.

The second event involved the decision makers, the group who needed to 'influence' events. The track of our path into the hurricane was indeed a smooth arc as we kept the wind on the beam and came in on the side of the hurricane. The barometer was beginning to plummet as we came closer to the eye. It was time to leave, to tack out and get that 'kick up the pants' to shoot out the back of the hurricane.

'OK, chaps, let's tack out. We've had enough of Michael. Time to leave.'

'Hang on,' said the man on the barometer, the man I had charged with monitoring the parameters to decide our fate. 'The barometer has some way to go yet.'

What fear?

But a little learning can be a dangerous thing and it was, indeed, time to go. Even though I had promised to abide by their call and not overrule their decision, I was not expecting to have to do so in quite the way I did.

Awareness of the power of motivation also came into play later in the race, when, having sailed over three-quarters of the way around the world, my team and I were becalmed off Madeira. We had sailed 32,000 miles over nine months. We found ourselves down in eighth place – but still with a chance of getting on the podium – and with only two legs left to go from Cape Town to La Rochelle before the final sprint back into Britain to a hero's welcome after an amazing, life-changing odyssey. As it happened we were doing very well. We left Cape Town with the wise words of South Africa's Bishop Desmond Tutu ringing in our ears, telling us that we were inspiring and full of courage – praise indeed from such a courageous, inspiring man. We always had brilliant starts, and, heading north, the whole fleet got becalmed before the Doldrums, which meant we started rationing food straight away. Food was going to be important now for the whole leg as we needed 5,000 calories a day. We were starving already and only ten days into a month-long leg to France..

We managed to get through the Doldrums. We all got out of there and no one had a big lead north or south, but the fleet split at Madeira. I jokingly say that I don't drink Madeira wine or eat Madeira cake and I've never been to Madeira, and nor will any of my family ever go for seven generations. (Since I said that, though, I have been and it's a very nice place.) A number of the fleet were going to the east of Madeira and the wind was coming from the northeast, so they were bashing into the wind. They were going slowly and making hard progress. Three of the fleet decided to go to the west of Madeira. Madeira is a very tall island with a big wind shadow stretching for 30 miles. There were three boats, ours lying third in that row, all within a few miles of each other, first, second and third in the race.

We were thinking, This is great, we'll get past Madeira, get the new wind first. The new wind further north comes from the west. We'll steam into La Rochelle, first, second or third, right on the podium for a final fantastic finish into Southampton.

Then, suddenly, my speedometer, the log, dropped to zero – three lemons, we called it, as the three-digit yellow display rang 0 – 0 – 0!

The boat stopped dead in the water. All around us, the 'white horses' on the breaking crests of the waves died back.

I looked ahead and the other two yachts were still bent to the breeze, cantering away. We had run into our own private wind hole. We were 45 miles downwind of Madeira and somehow, against all the knowledge I had, the wind had bounced, possibly for a second jump, high enough off the waves to leave us stranded.

For 16 hours we were totally and utterly impotent. The fleet marched on, but we remained. Even those struggling to break round Madeira to the east managed to free off and make good way. For 16 long, frustrating hours we tried everything we could to encourage the yacht to creep forward, but to no avail.

At one stage a supertanker was steaming towards us – 200,000 tons of oil in a thin steel membrane charging towards us at 20 knots. I actually called him on the radio and explained the situation: 'We've been racing around the world for eight and a half months, for 30,000 miles, and I can't move, I've got no wind. If I have to put on the engine it means I've got to retire. Can you alter course? The captain said he'd *try*, which was very nice of him! Clearly he did or I wouldn't be writing this book now. He missed us by a quarter of a mile, which at sea isn't that far at all. However, when the wind finally filled and we came out of the shadow of Madeira we were no longer in the same wind pattern as the fleet. As they charged up the coast of Africa doing around 12 knots (that's about 15 m.p.h.), all we could do was pick up the crumbs under the table. Every single day we lost another 100 miles to the fleet.

As the fleet rounded the top of Spain to enter the Bay of Biscay, they couldn't see Cape Finisterre because of the storms and the spray. For us it was like being on the *Mary Celeste*: we were completely fogbound and, again, with no wind. We were running out of food, and running out of time.

For the last few days we had been eating only porridge – all our other supplies were spent. Porridge is lovely with sugar or treacle or honey, but all we had to go with our porridge was Tabasco sauce. There are only so many ways you can cook porridge and Tabasco, and, trust me, we tried them all.

Crucially, we were running out of time to get into La Rochelle to join the start of the last leg of the race into Southampton.

This meant we wouldn't actually get into Southampton with the rest of the fleet.

There's a lot in this story now about motivation and understanding the motivations of different people, but also about trying to create a common vision and value. I guess that, from a leadership perspective, this was one of the biggest and most testing times. We weren't going to get into Southampton! Can you imagine? I'd had to paint the picture in my crew's minds that eleven boats would come home to a hero's welcome with friends, family, champagne, helicopters and television cameras, and a week later Team Large on Olympic Group (the name of our sponsor) would limp into a deserted Ocean Village in Southampton to see a fleet of locked-up boats, empty beer cans, tumbleweed and bemused locals. That just wouldn't be right.

The first element of trying to motivate a team effort, of resolving differences and gaining a collective commitment, is to settle on a unifying goal. Some of my team said, 'Come on, Manley, why don't we stop now and put the engine on? We'll get into La Rochelle, prepare ourselves for Leg 7, do really well in Leg 7. That way we, and the rest, will know we're good, because we *are* good.' (Putting on the engine disqualified you from that leg of the race – we would score zero points, but still be allowed to compete in the rest of the race – a big call!)

Other members of the team expressed their different viewpoints and said, 'No, we came to sail the whole way around the world. We don't want to put the engine on now. We want to keep going right until the last minute.' (We had already crossed our out-going track, so, technically, we had sailed all the way around the world already, but their perspective was on the purity of the sailing – and totally understandable.)

I had to hold a pragmatic view; it would be impossible for us to win the race now, so it became all about respect.

Somehow, I had to create a unifying position. I also knew that, in this instance, it wasn't a decision that was just mine: this was something so fundamental to the beliefs and values of all my team that we had to have a decision that we could all buy into. In my mind, I knew that this decision was so important to our long-term reflection on our own personal achievement in this race. I did not want, even 10 years down the line, one of my crew in the corner of a bar in some far-flung corner of the world to say, 'I didn't agree with that decision.' This was now out of my hands to direct, too important for me just to force my way. I would have to ensure that every single member of my crew was 'on board' with the next course of action. We had conflicting needs, motivations and requirements, but somehow we had to paint a common, unifying vision; once again, Nelson was to be my inspiration.

The picture I painted in the minds of my team was one of not coming in with the rest of the fleet, arriving to an empty marina, missing our friends and loved ones, who would have booked their tickets from all over the globe to welcome us home; too late for them now to change their travel arrangements. I asked my team how they would feel if our return, after nine months and 30,000 miles of sailing around the world 'the wrong way', was to be no more than a silent berth. I asked them all to reflect deeply on why they took part, what it was that had driven them to take the courageous step and invest a year of their lives in such an amazing endeavour. We spoke for a while, as a team and in smaller groups. Then I asked them to share what they wanted. The whole team were totally behind one simple goal: to arrive in England with the fleet. That was fantastic. Now all we had to do was work backwards from there. To come in with the rest of the fleet, we would have to leave La Rochelle at the same time as everyone else.

'Agreed?'

'Agreed!' was the unanimous response.

Currently, everyone else was already in La Rochelle enjoying the hospitality and food of northern France. Meanwhile, we were supping rancid water and still eating porridge with Tabasco.

Every day that we were out there still sailing while the other teams prepared themselves reduced our potential for success on what would be the last and toughest phenomenally competitive leg. Whether we wanted to win that last leg or not, we knew we had to allow ourselves 72 hours to recuperate before the race started, to give us any chance of being competitive. Planning back from La Rochelle, based on top speed under engine, this then meant that, if we weren't in a certain place by a certain time, we would have no option but to put on the engine. 'Do we all agree?' We did.

So what do you do next, after such an emotional debate and such a life-changing decision? How do you defuse the tension of relief and disappointment? Well, we were not racing, so, 'Hands to bathe!' The sea was crystal clear and as calm as a millpond, so we all leapt over the side and enjoyed the moment. There had to be a 'release' after such pressure. Mind you, you do not swim for long in water 3,000 metres deep – you're not sure what's looking up and thinking, 'Hmm, breakfast'.

As it happened, a few moments after we climbed back on board, towelled off and got back to sailing the boat, a 70-foot humpback whale surfaced almost alongside. Nature has a way of putting things into perspective. You may feel down and full of self-pity, but then it all pales into insignificance when you're alongside the majesty and awe of Mother Nature.

It was without doubt one of the hardest choices we all had to make, but that time did come when we had no option but to put on the engine. So we started the engine and sent a signal back saying we were retiring from Leg 6 and making best speed into La Rochelle with the intention of winning the final leg into Southampton.

When I looked at motivation in order to rally my team, I once again used McClelland's model, looking at achievement, affiliation and influence. Some of my team had to feel they could influence what was happening, and I let them do so. They were part of the planning, passage making and the organisation of what we had to do between now and La Rochelle. For others it was one of affiliation and having a strong team. I motivated those people by getting them to be the rallying call, the guys who would support those who were so disappointed, the ones who would look at the welfare of the team, rather than the planning of the task. And the planning of the next leg, with its complex navigation and meteorological demands, I left to those who wanted to achieve. We had to 'park' Leg 6 of this race.

When we had wind, we sailed well. Up to Madeira we were with the lead pack. We had the strength as individuals and as a team to bounce back. We knew we'd done as much as we possibly could on this leg, while still giving ourselves the chance to do exceptionally well on Leg 7.

Leg 7 worked brilliantly. It was immense. We had an amazing time, and it was the most intense sailing of my life. Four days with almost zero sleep and, after this incredible journey of nine months, as we rounded the bottom of the Isle of Wight for the very last time, there were six boats all battling for first place. We were one of them. As we rounded the edge of Poole Bay, there were only five boats fighting for first place and we were in that lead group. And, as we came through the narrows at Hurst Castle into the Solent, there were now only four boats, neck and neck, pushing each other to the limits to fight for the honour of topping the podium, and we were in the fight. The last two marks saw the first four boats finish within seconds and minutes of each other, and we were one of those boats. We came in fourth. We made a massive statement to the world, and to ourselves, that we could achieve and we could do so much. We were, after all, Team Large!

Our collective journey over, individually our next journey of reintegration just beginning. My, our, mission accomplished, motivations fulfilled, personal goals achieved!

I need to give a little explanation here concerning my attacking Hurricane Michael. With enormous respect to the other skippers and crews in the Challenge (most of whom, it has to be said, completed the circumnavigation in less time than I did), when, as I briefed my crew, I spoke of the other yachts 'running away from Hurricane Michael like frightened rabbits', I know that they would not have acted with such thought or motivation. Each of the skippers made a judgement call based on their experiences and their crews, and, with their values to the fore, took the course of action they did. A certain amount of fear would have been with us all. Fear in itself is fine and my belief is that not to feel fear means not to be concerned with or to value life. Each yacht weighed the balance between competition and survival and acted accordingly.

Incidentally, a few days after Hurricane Michael, we were confronted by Tropical Storm Nadine. Can you guess the 'storm strategy' of every one of the yachts now? Yup. All 12 attacked Nadine. Great lesson there on not resting on your laurels. Just because you have been successful once, it does not mean you can just repeat, as your competitors will have learned from your actions.

Key Learnings

- Self-interest drives our actions – remember the honey in the bough of the tree!

- Everyone has a unique balance of motivational needs – achievement, affiliation and influence – McLelland's Three Needs theory.

- Hurricane Michael – you set your attitude to influence the attitude of others – a threat is no more or less than an opportunity.

- Success needs to be improved upon – your competitors learn. One good storm strategy does not mean you can sit back on your laurels.

Notes

_____

_____

_____

_____

_____

_____

_____

_____

_____

_____

_____

_____

_____

_____

CHAPTER 7

WHO GIVES THE POWER?

Sometimes, trying to get others to do something, trying to influence them, just does not seem to work. Have you ever wondered how some people are able to persuade others to help them out, on a regular basis? How some people just 'get' other people, understand what they're thinking and build a rapport without even trying? Or so it seems. Trying to get others to do what you want or to see things your way is not easy, but it is key to achieving successful outcomes in relationships and leadership.

So far we have focused on the discovery element of being a Compassionate Leader – what lights the fire for Me, You and Us. So now let's look at how we apply it. This chapter will give you insights, stories and tools to help you to increase your power and influence, helping you to achieve what you need to succeed. This is as much about the skills required to be a Compassionate Leader as it is about the attitude.

This chapter exposes a profound shift in thinking on what 'power' and 'influence' actually are, where they come from, how to get them and how to use them. This will change your life – seriously. I am not being over dramatic on this; the impact of what I am about to share is profound. It certainly was for me!

Understanding power and influence is a key premise of Compassionate Leadership and can be applied in all walks of life: it is just as important in trying to influence an executive board as it is a sporting team or a reluctant teenager.

Frequently, there is a negative connotation with the word *power* and a more positive one associated with *influence*. This is not the reality. When I facilitate the questions 'What is power?' and 'What is influence?' at a conference, the delegates will respond and connect power with rank, position, status, force, cajoling, imposing and other negative or forceful aspects of ego and influence. For influence they suggest relating, persuading, working with, helping: an altogether kinder connection. But this thinking is flawed.

I can 'influence' you by trying to give you a Chinese burn or a knuckle rub, and that's not particularly positive! Likewise, I could be in a position of perceived 'power' and be jolly good to you, maybe by being first XV rugby captain on a winning streak with a great team feeling, and you'd deem that to be very positive.

In this chapter I explore the psychology behind power and influence and their impact on relationships and leadership. This creates a sea change in our understanding of power and influence as an UMU tool for all life's situations.

Power and leadership are interrelated. People will gravitate towards, and are influenced by, those who are powerful. Those who are powerful have followers whom they influence. I have found that leaders are powerful for many reasons, and this led me to question what power really is. Where does it come from? How is it that some individuals exude such a force that people want to be led by them and others struggle?

There has been so much written about influence and how to influence people and I believe that a lot of what has been written is fundamentally flawed. It just doesn't ring true. And judging by the number of invitations that come unsolicited for me and other leaders to attend various seminars entitled 'How to get your way', 'How to influence other people', it would appear that I am not alone in my quest to discover the Holy Grail of getting others to do my bidding!

Given the confusion in the materials I had read and my disconnect with common perceptions and beliefs, I did a lot of research on how to really understand power and influence and how to apply them. I looked at my own actions when I was able to influence, and when I have been totally unable to change another's actions or thinking.

Then a breakthrough happened that changed it all when I stumbled across a fantastic piece of research done in 1959 by a couple of social psychologists called John French and Bertram Raven. I want to explain this, not only because it is fundamental to my principles, and the principles of Compassionate Leadership, but also because, for me, it has been a life-changing revelation in my understanding of the principles of power and influence. The impact on my own leadership ability has been immense. The impact on my efficacy as a facilitator or coach has been dramatic. I've shared this research with many different organisations and groups, from large to small, all over the world, and the light bulb goes on in people's minds – they get it! It is truly staggering.

Other people have worked with French and Raven's 1959 research and looked at their theory and tried to improve on it and work with it. My view is that no one has got close to explaining how profound this research actually is and most of the modern attempts to explain power have, I believe, fallen well wide of the mark. It was, it is, without doubt, one of the most important and impactful papers on social power. There's much more information that you can get on this particular research than I will tell you in the book, of course, so please do continue your own studies if you're so inclined – I'm sticking to my UMU principle.

There are two basic premises to French and Raven's research.

The first is 'power is potential influence' and the second is 'influence is kinetic power'.

In other words, you cannot influence unless you have power!

This is a bold and controversial statement that reflects the partnership we spoke of earlier.

When I work with world leaders and introduce that statement, it is always illuminating how many people just cannot accept it; it is too remote from their current perceptions. If you are in that category, then, suspend your disbelief for a moment and let me talk you through it.

The second premise of French and Raven's work relates to where power comes from. Who gives you the power? Where do you get it from? What is your 'base of power', your 'power base'?

A rank or a position is not a base of power in its own right, and in a minute I'll take you through the main bases that French and Raven identified.

The ground-breaking realisation from French and Raven's work is that it is the people that you are trying to influence who actually give you your base of power.

It is a real eye opener and can be quite shocking when you realise what you have been doing. It comes down to the saying 'A leader gets the team they deserve.' Sounds harsh, but, in essence, it is right. Have a look at your team. Reflect now on how committed or compliant they are to your requests.

This is because, in reality, influence is about a partnership. In other words, I can't influence you unless you allow me to influence you. Hold onto that. We cannot just zoom past that statement. It is absolutely fundamental to understanding how we are to influence others – in other words, fundamental to how we are to be leaders.

I can't influence you unless you allow me to influence you.

That is such a big statement. It is brilliant. Hang on in there and the light bulb will come on!

With no particular religious comment to make here – although religion does explain quite well – let us look at God, the Pope and Catholics, and we will throw in a Buddhist for good measure.

According to belief, God gives the Pope his position, but it isn't God who gives him his power: it's the Catholics whom the Pope influences. It is the Catholics who say to the Pope, 'I believe in you, and what you represent, therefore you may influence me.' So let's look at the relationship with the Pope and the Buddhist. The Pope's 'position' has not changed one bit, but his ability to influence has changed dramatically. He cannot influence the Buddhist, as the Buddhist has not given him the permission, the power base, to do so.

It's a simplified argument, but you get my point.

So, you may have a position, but it is the people you influence who give you the power, the 'permission' to influence.

This challenges our understanding of where the 'power' actually lies or comes from. A Republican will not be influenced by the British Queen, but I am. Her 'position' is the same, but our acceptance is different. The power lies within the 'influencee' (for want of a better word).

I can summarise the last few paragraphs by saying: , 'You cannot influence unless you have power.' And, *It is the people that you are trying to influence who actually give you power.*

This really is chunky and exciting stuff. I love it, but I do need to go into more detail to help your understanding and acceptance.

The five bases of power

Let's look at the bases of power that French and Raven identified. There are five, and I'll look at them by first explaining what the base of power is. Then I'll give the reason why it's a base of power, and we'll discuss the outcome in terms of whether it creates a commitment to or a compliance with the desired course of action. We'll also look at how you can strive to 'be given' that power base, if you so wish.

French and Raven's five power bases are:

- reward
- coercion
- expert
- referent
- legitimacy

Reward and coercion

The first two power bases are reward and coercion; they go hand in hand. These are about being able to bestow a positive or negative outcome on the person you are trying to influence. Both are more than likely to lead to compliance, and only a superficial change in the person, leaving their privately held beliefs, attitudes and values unchanged. Essentially, these power bases create a 'transaction' between the parties.

Obviously coercion would lead to compliance because people aren't buying into what it is that you are influencing them to do, just carrying out a duty knowing that, if they don't do it, then there's a negative outcome. Let's use an example. If you're trying to persuade a small child to put on their seatbelt in the car and say, 'Put your seatbelt on or you'll go to bed early,' they have not 'bought into' the putting-on of a seatbelt. The likelihood is that you will need to threaten again the next time they get into the car!

A cycle of behaviour develops whereby a threat is needed to complete the action. There will always need to be a coercive element. So using coercion as a power base may well get the act done, but in a compliant way that will need further supervision and, therefore, time and more coercion later on

Or you could say, 'Put your seatbelt on and I'll buy you an ice cream.' Clunk-click! But that will need a lot of ice creams in the future.

There is a key problem with both these power bases. If at any stage the people you are trying to influence believe that you cannot, or will not, actually coerce or reward, the power base will be whipped from under your feet. The first time the kid does not get the ice cream, no clunk-click. The first time you do not follow through with the early bedtime, then, uh-oh, no go next time! The Western political rhetoric around acts of aggression by other states does not deter, as the belief that the West will actually do something is low. If I do not believe that you could or would give me a knuckle rub, then you will not be able to influence me from a power base of coercion as I won't give it to you!

So how would you 'earn' these power bases (assuming you want to)? It's easy! Just do it. For coercion, just threaten your way through life, and for reward, just bribe! That sounds harsh, but it's true; if you have not created a higher sense of purpose with your sales team, then the transaction of a sales bonus – the reward power base – is the only one available to you.

I really do not believe that one would consciously strive to be given these power bases. I do believe that, if we are unconscious of our actions and find ourselves in a directive corporate culture, we behave in such a way that these are the power bases we end up with. Company bonus schemes, performance review processes and commissions create the necessary 'transactional' environment whereby the default power base given to the leadership is that of reward or coercion. Parental bribery with ice creams, sweets and other treats also creates that 'transactional' space, and I believe that, if we are not careful and conscious of what we're doing, many aspects of our formal society and religious convictions of promise or pain create a compliance to 'good' and a compliance away from 'bad'.

Expert, referent and legitimacy

These next three are power bases associated with an outcome of commitment.

Expert

Let's take the 'expert' one first. This is about knowledge, and the other's belief that you have that knowledge. If I believe that you know what you're talking about, that you are the expert, then I will give you the power base of being an expert. You can influence me.

A fantastic example of this is the film *Flight of the Phoenix*, set in World War Two. (You ought to watch this anyway – it's a classic.) A transport plane is heading south into Africa and crashes deep in the Sahara desert. The soldiers are too far away to walk for help. No one knows they're there as they were flying with radio silence. They are not exactly sure where they are themselves. Their only chance of survival is to rebuild the plane.

One of the team, an older, bespectacled man, pipes up and says, 'Well, I build planes.'

The others are ecstatic. Redemption! Survival! Congratulating themselves on their fortune, the say, 'Fantastic! Great! We'll do whatever you say, just tell us what you need.'

They follow this chap as he's helping them build the plane. The desert is a hive of activity, sawing, hammering, drawings and rulers. Then, over a cup of coffee one of them asks, 'So what was the last plane you built?'

The chap explains, 'It was a Spitfire. About four feet long, and I painted it all myself. It was my finest model.'

'What? You have never actually built a proper plane? You're a model-plane builder?'

He protests, saying the principles of flight are the same, it is just a difference of scale. But it is no good. The work stops. Depression, disaster, arguments, anger.

They won't obey anything he says because, now, they don't believe he has the knowledge. In their eyes he can no longer hold the power base of 'expert', so he cannot influence them. But, for our model-plane builder, nothing has actually changed.

It is a classic example of where power bases come from.

Originally the crew 'gave' him the power base of being an 'expert'. Likewise they took that power base away. While he had the power base, he could influence them. But, when he didn't have it, he could not. In the film, the leader comes along and prophetically says, 'In the land of the blind, the one-eyed man is king. Let's follow this chap as it's the best chance we have.' The people agree and give him his power base back again, and . . . Well, I won't ruin it for you.

However, it is worth noting that there are potential pitfalls with being given an 'expert' power base. First, it can lead to a fairly directive style of leadership. If someone believes they are the expert, they will tend to 'tell' others how to do a task, because they know how to do it. 'Expert' leaders may refrain from soliciting and accepting feedback or suggestions on how the task could or should be done because they may see that as a potential risk to their power base as an 'expert'. I mention this so that you can be aware of it, if you are an expert in your field, so you can lead in a manner that still allows people to engage.

Second, another problem with having an 'expert' power base is that, if another expert walks into the room, and the people believe the new person is more of an expert, they can transfer their power base to the new person and away from you. Your power base is fickle and transient. There is always that danger and it is something to be aware of if you need to influence a group of people to achieve a particular task.

A parent trying to establish an 'expert power base' may well say, 'The reason you should put your seatbelt on is so that, if I have to brake really hard, you don't fly through the windscreen and hurt yourself.' Fair call, sounds reasonable, and Mum and Dad know what they are talking about, so on the seatbelt goes. The child can accept the 'expert reasoning' and will end up being committed to wearing a seatbelt, and it's a case of clunk-click every trip. Sounds better, doesn't it? Incidentally, this is yet another example of the efficacy of that 'early investment' in effort I spoke about to gain commitment instead of trying to force compliance: rather than just bellowing, 'Put your seatbelt on!', a reasoned discussion taking a few minutes on the first occasion saves loads of time later!

Of course, to have any chance of earning this power base, you may well have to be good at something! Or, as the name suggests, an 'expert'. So go to school, read, study, experiment, do and learn; then, eventually, you may earn the badge.

Or, and this is one of the overriding realities of this thinking, just put on a convincing show that you do actually know what you are doing, and you may get away with it – until you are found out! Remember it is the 'belief' that you are the expert that is so important, not that you actually are! (Interestingly, in a recent survey of the main fears of top executives by the American management consulting firm McKinsey and Co., 'being found out' was right up there.)

Referent

Let's now take the referent power base. This one is all about identifying with the leader, and I like to affectionately call it the 'Beckham' power base. If David Beckham wears a sarong (as he did/does), those who identify with Beckham also start wearing a sarong – just because they identify, or want to identify, with him. A new tattoo for David? Guess I'll have one, too! It is about their personality and, if you're the leader, it's about your personality, your character; it might also be about your value set, how you act and how people look on you as a role model and want to identify with you. This leads to commitment, as people are buying into the identity of the referent leader and aspiring to be like them. They see either a present or a desired self within the other.

By the way, just in case you catch me at home on a sunny day or on the beach, let me just say that I've been wearing a sarong since Beckham was wearing nappies! But David

Beckham has influenced me in many other ways; I believe he is a hugely impressive character who has managed to stay grounded throughout all the fame and attention, and being grounded is definitely one of my aspirations!

Again, be careful with aspiring to be given this power base. If the team sniff any lack of authenticity then the referent base vanishes. I remember when I was a junior officer in the Royal Navy, doing rounds of the ship. I would visit and inspect all the different departments that I was responsible for and talk to the chaps to see how they were. Sometimes they would ask, 'Which football team do you support, sir?' I could easily have suggested one, but, actually, I am a bit of a rugby man and not so keen on soccer (I like the game, just don't like the attitude of the top-level players). So I would tell them so. Other junior officers would be heard to say, 'Oh, yes, I tend to follow Arsenal United, don't you know?' If you try too hard for a referent base you may well end up trying to be too chummy and lose your authenticity. Be yourself and be the best yourself you can be. And if, when you are at your very best, your team aspire to 'identify' with you, 'refer' to you, then that won't be a bad thing.

This is an interesting one. To be given this power base, you must be 'you'. You cannot pretend to be anything you are not – not without a massive, conscious and consistent effort. But what you can do – and I speak about this when dealing with motivation – is to be aware of the characters of the people you are trying to influence and use their language – former UK Prime Minister Tony Blair was very good at doing this!

Legitimacy

The power base of legitimacy derives from the ultimate belief that you have a right to influence me. This is the one to aspire to. This is the power base that can lead to long-lasting commitment to your influence. But it is also the one that takes the most effort to be given. As with all things in life, there is no such thing as a free lunch.

This power base is clearly demonstrated in our discussion on God, the Pope, Catholics and the Buddhist. The Catholics absolutely believe in the Pope and the Pope's absolute legitimate right to influence them, and so they follow his every proclamation. Non-Catholics – the Buddhist, for example – will look at the Pope differently. They may well respect him, admire him, consider him to be an expert on matters spiritual, but, crucially, they do not give him that legitimacy, so the Pope cannot influence them as he can Catholics. I am not a Catholic. I am sure the Pope is a top chap with pure intent and huge spiritual awareness but I would not put him on my list of people who can wield influence over me.

Clearly, if the people you are trying to influence believe that you *should* be influencing them, they'll be committed to whatever you want them to do. This belief in you *allows* you to influence. It can become an expectation that you *do* influence. With the people's belief, you will influence them even if that is not your intent – it is up to them.

If the child in the back of the car believes that Mum and Dad have their best interests at heart then the chances are they will not be too much of an issue with wearing their seat-belt (though they may need reminding of that unconditional love from time to time!).

So how do you actually gain that legitimacy?

How do you get people to believe that you have a legitimate right to influence them? That you should and must do so? How do you retain that legitimacy? The idea comes up throughout this book and is at the heart of being that Compassionate Leader.

In this scenario, there is no substitute for time and effort. Over time you build relationships, build trust, allow people to see how you act as a role model, and to see how you act with other people. By effort and consciousness, you can earn that badge. This can lead to a virtuous circle: I allow you to influence me and I see that it benefits me, so I'll happily let you influence me some more – and so the legitimacy grows.

The legitimate power base is the one that a Compassionate Leader strives for!

We saw this in the illustration of Aesop's fable in my chapter on motivation – 'What Lights my Fire?'. There is self-interest in the farmer's ultimate wish to preserve the tree, because now he derives benefit from it, due to his liking for honey. A key understanding in being given a legitimate power base is that, if your team can see their self-interest reflected in your leadership, they'll allow you to lead. So legitimacy is the ultimate one to go for and the power base of a Compassionate Leader.

We also saw this with the leader's intervention in the story that illustrated the expert power in *The Flight of the Phoenix*: when the team had taken away the expert power base from the model-plane maker, it was the leader, whom the men held in high regard, who was able to restore that power base; the men held him in a 'legitimate' power base and trusted his judgement; through him, their self-interest was being met.

So to be given this power base demands that you, authentically, have a desire to secure the best *for* your people as well as the best *out of* them, that you do have their best interests at heart and genuinely desire to build trust in the relationship. Essentially, steer your ship towards Compassionate Leadership.

If you now apply this ground-breaking thinking of French and Raven to all the other parts of this book, you will see that every aspect of the book and the whole concept of Compassionate Leadership is about working to be given that legitimacy to lead, to influence, to relate.

Remember that it is the people you're trying to influence who give you your power base. You cannot demand it, and you must work to build relationships that bring about this happy outcome.

An extra power base: information

Later on, French and Raven did discover one extra power base: information. But it has a different slant to it from the others. The difference is that it isn't about the belief in the person who is trying to influence, but belief in the relevance and validity of the information itself; the power lies with the information, not the person.

If, for example, I have in my pocket a picture of you with a donkey and a water melon, then this will allow me to influence you. It gives me a certain amount of power over you in terms of how I might intend to use this picture. However, if I pass on the picture to another, then your concern about its use, and therefore your ability to be influenced, lies not now with me, but with the new holder of the picture. You have transferred the information power base from me to the other. If the picture is now posted on Facebook, then the 'power base' sits with no one. No one can influence you through their exclusive possession of the information. I can no longer influence you and I no longer have the information power.

(Relax, it was just a Greek shopping trip!)

Another, more business-focused, example that I witnessed was when a certain large printer and product company bought an equally large IT services company. Product Co., as we'll call it, had its own systems and procedures that it wanted to integrate. There was an individual who used to work with Product Co., and who now worked for IT Serv Co., who knew all the Product Co. systems in advance of everyone else. Without doubt the influence he could exert over many people over the first year was due to the information knowledge he had, and, boy, did that person try to maximise his influence! It did not last long, of course, for, as the two companies integrated further, the information became common knowledge and the power base disappeared, as did this chap's ability to influence others.

Stop and think

If you're struggling to influence somebody, stop and think. What power base have they given you? If they haven't given you a power base, then you cannot influence them. Neither can you demand that they give you a power base. What you can do is work to build that relationship so they could potentially give you one of the power bases that lead to commitment.

Be it at home, at school, at work or on the local am-dram committee, if no one is listening to your ideas or input, then consider what power base you have.

Now that we've covered the theory behind power and influence, let's look at how it can be applied in our everyday lives. I will tell a story!

In another large IT organisation that I worked with, many staff had been transferred from a civil-service career into the private sector when the contracts were outsourced. One of the young leaders in the IT organisation was really struggling. No matter how hard he tried, he could not get this group to do what he asked. Somehow, without any outward sign of rebellion, nothing would actually change.

I spoke to him about what power base these transferred individuals had given him. Could he *reward* or *coerce* them? No, he couldn't, because he wasn't in a position to pay them more or less, promote or sack them. Did they think he had a *legitimate* right to influence them? No they did not – he was a whipper-snapper, a money-grabbing private sector chap!

Could they *refer* with him? No they couldn't because he was a young chap in private industry and they were slightly more mature people in the civil service who'd held their jobs for many years and knew them inside out. And there were big cultural differences between the two to resolve as well.

Did they think that he was an *expert*? No, they didn't, thank you. They knew their jobs inside out.

So this person had no option. He could not influence them. Shout, cajole, enthuse, inform? Nope, not a thing would work without their giving him a power base. He had no option but to play the long game, to invest time in building the relationships.

Perhaps some people in the group could identify with him. He played hockey. Maybe someone else played hockey in that group. Maybe he could build a relationship with that person and use them to spread his influence.

Perhaps he needed to make sure they understood that he was an expert in *his* role, not an expert in *theirs*, but could nonetheless give them the direction and support they needed to do the best they could. That he was an expert leader, in other words.

He would have to spend the time to try to get them to realise that they could fulfil their self-interest through him. If he could raise the belief that he had their best interests at heart, he might achieve the 'legitimacy' he needed.

This chap had no option but to make a concerted and conscious effort to try to be given a power base in order to be able to influence.

This is not easy stuff. But I hope that the light bulb is shining brightly now.

Now consider your reluctant teenager.

In their eyes, you know nothing and they and their friends know everything. Expert? No. There is no way they can relate to you. And be careful (dads especially) in trying to, like, relate, man – it ain't cool, wicked, epic. Like, you know nuffin' and don't dig. (Or whatever language it is.) Referent? No!

The legitimacy that came with early years of unconditional love has evaporated too. Legitimate? No!

To reward or coerce? Hmm! That just creates a reluctant transaction and will cost you either way – in bribes or broken furniture and slammed doors. It's expensive, short-term and hard work.

Somehow, you will need to spend the time and effort and

'sell' in a controlled, emotionally intelligent and 'compassion-ate' way the idea that you have their best interests at heart, that your intention is for their self-worth to be fulfilled and that, even though it is a different world, you are not a complete numpty – and all the while being acutely aware of your own emotions and body language, and also theirs. It's the Me, You and Us model.

A good way to approach this might be by following the example of a very wise, local chief I spent some time with in the delta regions of Nigeria. He was compelled to force the horrible task of relocation for the whole of his community as the extraction of oil had caused his village to sink. I wanted to know the secret of his leadership as, all around me, I could see total commitment to the task in hand from all the villagers, young and old alike. So what was it? He told me, 'Manley, first I listen' and that was it! Love it!

If people have given you that legitimate power base, in order to use it you need to make sure that what you're offering is what that person needs. Let's consider Hurricane Michael, which I took my team into during the BT Global Challenge. Let's look at what power base the team had given me.

Clearly, although I was the captain, I couldn't reward or coerce. There was no way I could offer them any benefit for letting me influence them. They were crew volunteers. They had paid to take part.

Nor could I make them walk the plank, for those days are long gone, (sighs), which isn't necessarily a bad thing, either. So that left three power bases that they could have given me to allow me to influence them to such a degree that people who have never sailed before in their lives were happy to follow and be influenced into attacking a hurricane: expert, referent and legitimacy.

Let's take the one of 'expert' first. Was I an expert in hurricanes? It was important as we approached the storm that the team should look at me with confidence and believe I knew what I was doing. So, as I was briefing them on the hurricane, I was calm and spoke knowledgeably. In many respects that would help them to give me an 'expert' power base, so they would think, Manley knows a lot about hurricanes; I'm safe sailing with him; I'll let him influence me. If only they'd known the truth that it was actually *my* first hurricane as well.

So, potentially, some of them could have given me an 'expert' power base.

But could any of them identify with me – that 'referent' power base? Possibly, yes. Remember the story of how I used David McClelland's Three Needs Theory to tap into the motivational needs of all the crew? The achievers would have 'referred' to 'Let's attack Hurricane Michael, and let's come out in first place.' For those members of the crew, that first place was important – the concept of doing well and succeeding in the race rather than just sailing around the world. Using the words and choosing a strategy to help them to come in first would help them to identify with me.

For the affiliators I used words and phrases that made them relate to me as a team player – 'we', 'Team Large', 'I believe in you', 'together' …

And for the influencers, we worked on understanding the parameters together. Collectively we could 'group' around influencing the outcome. I allowed them to make the key decisions.

So the whole crew may well have 'identified' with or 'referred' to me and that could have been the power base they gave me that allowed me to influence them.

Or they may have given me the 'legitimacy' power base, after gaining the experience they had of me over the previous four or five months: living my life true to my own values, looking after their best interests, surviving various storms and arriving in one piece in Boston, sharing experiences and adventures along the way. Over that period they had seen how I'd dealt with them and with other people, how I always strove to be that Compassionate

Leader. The power base they gave me of 'legitimacy' allowed commitment to be the outcome, so as a result of that we were committed to attacking Hurricane Michael, and more.

So rank, position, title and status are not sources of power. You do not inherit a power base: you earn it. Power is a positive, but it is how you use it that might be perceived in a negative manner.

Money

So what about money? Surely money gives you power? If you have money, you can do anything you wish and demand that everybody obey your every wish too. Let's look more closely at that and apply French and Raven's research.

Let's say that you are Mr Rich and you want me to do something for you. You want to influence my actions. How are you going to do that? 'Manley, do what I say and I will pay you handsomely'? Or 'Manley, do what I say or else you won't get paid a cent'? Hmm, all I see there are 'reward' and 'coerce'. But if I do not believe either that you will pay me or that you won't, then you have the same power base in my eyes as a tramp – your money is worthless. It is useful in getting your way only if you weald it. If Warren Buffett says 'jump', why should I jump – unless he was going to pay me to jump (reward), or fire me from his employ (coerce)?

Money can help. It could lead to a commitment if I could see the realisation of my self-worth through it. But, essentially, it could give you the transactional compliance you deserve only through wielding reward or coercion.

But it may be that I respect Mr Buffet, that I think he has my best interests at heart, that he is looking after me by asking me to jump, so I *will* jump, because in my belief I have given him a legitimate right to influence me. It was not the money that enabled his influence: it was my belief in his character and intent.

So you see, money, in itself, is not 'power'. You can influence me only by using it. Or, as we said right at the start, power is potential influence, and influence is kinetic power.

So if you are reading this book and it has influenced you, what power base did you give me?

Influence

Beyond this superb work on power by French and Raven, there was work done by many different people, including the likes of psychologists David Kipnis, Stuart Schmidt and Ian Wilkinson in 1980, and before that Kipnis in 1976. They all tried to discover what means of influence people use. There are a number of categories that I'll mention here:

Means of influence:
- assertiveness
- ingratiation
- rationality
- sanctions
- exchange
- upward appeal
- blocking
- coalitions

Let's think about these categories a little more. Do these 'means of influence' link to commitment or compliance? It is not straightforward in that much of this is so relevant to the situation that you find yourself in and the power base you have been given. So the key thing about 'means of influence' is that we use the right means for the right person in the right moment.

However, *assertiveness* sounds as if it could well be leading to compliance, particularly if it is used to force you to do something. But, if you have given me a legitimate power base, I could be assertive and still maintain that power base and that commitment. However, if I kept on being assertive, after a while you would remove that legitimacy as you stopped seeing the fulfilment of your self-worth.

Ingratiation is really about appealing to the character of that person. We have a negative connotation with the word *ingratiate*: it sounds as if someone is smarming up to someone else. But what we're actually trying to do is help to build and share 'identity', so, again, that can lead to commitment.

Rationalising is about working with people's intellect and reasoning in a logical and unemotional way. Interestingly here, if I'm a rational person, then rationalising with me would work. If I'm more of an emotional person, then rationalising wouldn't work. If I'm emotional, don't rationalise with me: ingratiate with me instead. It may work.

Sanctions implies that compliance may be an outcome as it would go hand in hand with coercion as the power base. 'Do that or else . . . '

Likewise with *exchange*, which is just using a positive sanction rather than a negative one, though it would tend to lead to a 'transactional' agreement and hence compliance with coercion as the power base.

Upward appeal is realising people's benefits in a higher order, so it's getting people to realise they can move up if they work with this person and this will more than likely lead to a commitment as self-interest can be fulfilled.

Blocking is what it is by definition. If there is a policeman standing in front of you wanting you to drive down one road and not the other, well that's blocking. Now, are you going to be compliant or committed? It depends on which power base you've given the policeman. If you think he's got a legitimate right to influence you, because he's looking after your welfare, then you'll happily go down the road he's asking you to go down. If, on the other hand, you're thinking, Why is the policeman telling me this? and you have a lawless outlook, you may do it reluctantly or refuse to do it at all.

The final means of influence I want to talk about – and in the modern world of networking this is critical – is that of *coalitions*, or how you can use the power of the people and the power of networks to spread your influence. This is demonstrated in the example I gave earlier of the young man trying to influence the group of public-sector personnel who had been acquired by a private organisation. He was trying to create coalitions with individuals within that grouping in order to exert influence.

The final part of the application of this theory is about whether the influence is soft or hard, depending on the person's ability to yield and choose to be influenced. So all the time when I'm using sanctions or assertion as a means of influence, then that is pretty hard. If I'm using reasoning, ingratiation or upward appeal, then that is soft. I believe that the soft tactics allow the person more freedom to decide either to yield or resist the influence attempt than the hard methods and so can lead to the ownership of the course of action they 'choose'. Hard methods have their place but be wary of continuous or frequent 'hard' usage as that then is perceived as a behavioural norm and may lead to loss of a commitment power base.

Key learnings

- Power and leadership are interrelated as both enable influence. Leadership involves influencing others, and ... you cannot influence unless you have a base of power.

- So power is potential influence and influence is kinetic power.

- People you are trying to influence will give you your power base. You cannot give it to yourself. If you have not been given a power base, you cannot influence them.

⟶

- Reward and coercion power bases are likely to lead to an outcome of compliance.

- Legitimacy, referent and expert power bases can lead to commitment.

- Applying the means of influence and the Power Use Model can change the level of commitment and compliance.

EXERCISE: POWER BASES

I'd like you to take some time out at this point and think about the power bases that have been given to you, and those that affect you.

Look at all the teams and individuals you are leading or influencing. How successful are you? Are there pockets of resistance or compliance? Have you gained full commitment?

Now look at those different groups and try to assess which power base you have been given by each.

Where you see reward or coercion, consider what you will need to do to gain a power base that is likely to lead to commitment.

Review the power bases above and write down when and how you've used that source of power in the past. To what outcome?

Review the means of influence you might prefer or tend to use.

Think about the people who have power and influence over you. What sources of power have you given them and why?

How could you work to be given a more effective power base?

Here's a grid with some examples that might help.   ⟶

Team	Committed or compliant	Evidence	Power base	Action
Project Bravo	Compliant	Low productivity, seem flat, high absenteeism.	Possibly none, but at best, coercion.	One-to-one with team leader, increase my visibility, discussion to understand and address concerns.
Blue Team	Committed	Excited, good results.	Legitimate. The team leader is always present and with the team. I have regular dialogues with her.	Carry on, but make sure we learn. Possibly team with Project Bravo

Notes

_____

_____

_____

_____

_____

_____

_____

_____

_____

_____

_____

_____

_____

_____

CHAPTER 8

BALANCE

Compassionate Leadership is about long-term, sustainable activity. It is not a 'quick fix', though much of what it is does have an immediate impact as well. It is about gaining long-term commitment.

But, to create longevity of leadership, sustained high performance and a committed as opposed to a compliant team, a leader must balance the needs between achieving the task, building the team and developing the individual. This chapter shows how this is possible, providing a memorable story and useful tools to ensure success.

Compassionate Leadership is about legacy. What legacy do you want?

The temptation when faced with a demanding, high-pressure or threatening situation is that we focus entirely on the task itself – just get your head down and soldier on. The pressure of the 'task' takes over our whole world, blanking out the needs of those around us and, eventually, blanking out our own needs too.

We stop being the master of the task and, instead, the task masters us. We become consumed by the need to deliver, at all costs, ignoring the development of individuals within the team, including ourselves, and being ignorant as to how well the team are actually working together, disregarding the efficacy of having a strong team. We tend to lose our sense of perspective.

Intense pressure has a similar physiological effect on us as fear, in that it releases adrenalin in the body; the blood leaves the head to feed the muscles ready for freeze, fight or flight; we stop thinking rationally. We become busy fools hacking away at the tree with a blunt axe.

A high-pressure, task-focused culture puts us into conflict as we operate far removed from our core value set.

Our corporate world is all about 'delivering the task'. The pressure is immense to answer to the City on a quarterly basis, and frequently to the detriment of long-term, more strategic considerations and investments, and invariably at the expense of the welfare and happiness of the people involved.

Cost cutting, redundancies, always being asked to do more with less. The first budget to be cut is the 'discretionary' spend on building teams and developing individuals. But I totally disagree with that perspective. Such things are not discretionary: they are *core*. Think about it. This is precisely the time when we need to develop the individuals and build them into a strong team. I may call it Compassionate Leadership, but in reality it is common sense. Not to do it means we will be stuck in a self-fulfilling cycle of forever working harder and harder. You can 'burn the furniture' for only so long before you run out of places to sit.

The relentless drive to deliver will not decrease, but only increase, so how are we to break this cycle? We are constantly having to do more with less.

Have the courage to embrace the philosophy of Compassionate Leadership and this so-called task-focused leadership, the tough image of 'deliver at all costs', will be exposed for the sham it is – an inefficient and short-term sham too! There can be only two endings to the current philosophy of 'deliver at all costs': goal failure and personal implosion.

Catastrophic failure. Not failure you can learn from, but failure that creates a desert.

Tragically, this thinking is everywhere. It is not just at work: it is at home, too.

Having survived the corporate onslaught of the day, we stagger home, punch-drunk, and are bombarded by more requests for our time. There are jobs to do around the house, and the children want a slice of us, too. We will be pushed for time to such a degree that we say no to our young child's offer to help us fix the shed, but at what cost? What is our wider role as a parent? What is our legacy? 'I have a shed to fix, I'll play with you later.' But, if we apply the principle of balancing needs – and, therefore, balancing our effort between achieving the task, building the team and developing the individual – then surely every task is an opportunity to fulfil our wider role of being a parent. Every little job can be seen as an investment in our legacy, potentially.

I have spoken much in this book about motivation and about fulfilling self-worth and how these enable commitment. We contemplated the performance benefits of commitment and the 'return on our investment' when we spend time gaining that commitment, as opposed to driving compliance, and the cost to business, ourselves and our people in that compliance. This balance of awareness, effort and time between achieving the task, building the team and developing the individual is exactly how you gain that commitment.

Abraham Lincoln summed it up nicely when he said, 'Give me six hours to chop down a tree and I will spend the first four sharpening the axe.'

And he was a clever chap!

Think about it? Are you hacking away at the tree with a blunt axe? Head down, headlong into action?

Almost without fail, when I work with teams in bonding, building or developing and use an experiential element in the programme, the delegates, having been briefed on all the requirements and parameters and briefed on the principles of gaining commitment and working effectively and efficiently as a team, make their first 'act' just that: action. No axe sharpening. Just straight in!

I remember when I was under training in the Royal Hong Kong Marine Police. We were given practical leadership tasks to complete. Each of us young inspectors was given the opportunity to lead. On one particular occasion, deep in the New Territories in the wild countryside around a reservoir, a particular young chap, who we knew had a tendency to 'act first', was taken aside for his briefing. His scenario was that, just over the horizon on the reservoir, a group of Chinese fishermen were about to embark on a spot of 'fish bombing', the highly illegal and extremely dangerous method of fishing whereby a detonator is strapped to a rock, set off then lobbed in the water killing all waterborne life in the vicinity. His briefing was detailed and precise. He was advised of the number of fishermen, their location and equipment, with a final reminder on the basic principles of leadership. The chap thought for a moment, then came running over to us, waving his arms and shouting, 'They're bombing the fish, go!' We did. In all directions. Classic!

Stop, before you start

There is a biological reason for this too, as, under stress, we engage the primitive part of our brain (sometimes called our 'lizard brain') which is all about fight, flight or freeze. But, if we can stop, count to 10 and let our neocortex – our developed brain – have a go, we can override our instinctive actions and act appropriately. The impulse to act is called the amygdala hijack – our reasoning rational self gets hijacked by the lizard!

Everybody reading this book will say that they are busy. That they don't have time for all this other stuff. The pressure to deliver is just too much. They can't stop.

I'm going to argue that what you cannot afford to do is to ignore the bigger picture, and that, if you make that investment in building a team and developing the individuals within, achieving any task will be simpler and more effective. You cannot afford *not* to stop.

I am also going to argue that, for longevity of leadership, for sustained high performance and to create a committed as opposed to a compliant team, for you to be a Compassionate Leader, you must balance the needs between achieving the task, building the team and developing the individual.

Remember the graph on commitment versus compliance from right at the beginning of the book about your return on investment? Well, this chapter gives you the framework to make that happen.

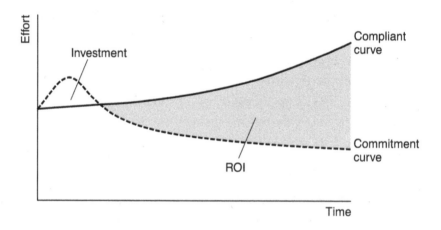

Figure 8.1 Commitment vs compliance

The philosophy I am about to share has had a profound impact on my life in so many ways. I was first introduced to it back in the early eighties as a young officer under training at the Britannia Royal Naval College in Dartmouth, England. It was here that so much of who I am now was formed. I learned to set my attitude to 'enjoy' the 05.30 'Early Morning Activities' of marching in freezing horizontal sleet, boat handling in the dark of midwinter and early-morning PT – if they wanted to 'test' me, then they would have to push really hard! It was here that I first learned the real meaning of camaraderie and what phenomenal power it gives you.

It was also the beginning of my transition into manhood. I

believe I was a late developer (mentally) in this respect and struggled with responsibility and application while at university. It was also at Dartmouth, during the studies on leadership, that I was first introduced to the British academic and leadership theorist John Adair's superb model of 'Action Centred Leadership' – a life-changing event, even though I may not have seen it that way at the time.

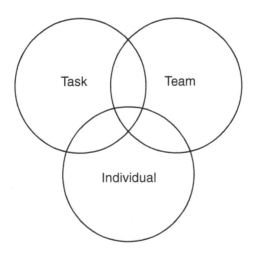

Figure 8.2 John Adair's model of Action Centred Leadership

This is another one of those truly fundamental concepts that form the foundation of Compassionate Leadership. It is superb! This next story was a profoundly moving and emotional part of my race around the world. It is one that changed me and my team for ever. It is one that made me so proud of my team and a story that helped me then, and now, in setting a sense of perspective.

Before I embarked on the life-changing journey of the BT Global Challenge, I consciously reminded myself of the power of John Adair's model. It proved to be a vital element of my leadership toolbox and a big differentiator among the fleet. There was good reason that we were known as the 'most popular of crews' as we managed to balance the needs of all and maintain the enjoyment of racing around the world.

My crew were special and I will tell you more about how we got together in the next chapter, but by the time we had reached Buenos Aires in Argentina we were a strong, bonded and highly effective team. However, this next leg was going stretch us all in so many ways. This was our first venture into the Southern Ocean, the mighty expanse of ferocious open ocean with unrelenting storms circling the globe. The beauty and majesty are matched by the cacophony and confusion of the seas.

Let me set the scene: As we left beautiful Buenos Aires with its warm and welcoming climate and people, we were far removed from the scale of the voyage we were about to embark on. Battling out of the River Plate, we pushed south until we reached the 'Land of Fire', Tierra del Fuego, and battled our way against the prevailing winds and seas around Cape Horn, whose name itself strikes fear in the heart of sailors and landlubbers alike! Having survived the tempestuous seas of the Cape, where the mighty winds and waves are funnelled and forced to their extreme by the closing of the land masses of Antarctica and South America, we then battled across more than 6,000 miles of untethered oceans towards the welcoming islands of New Zealand and the embrace of Wellington, dropping south through the Roaring Forties, the Furious Fifties and the Screaming Sixties to skim the top of the Antarctic circle, just above the zone of icebergs and growlers ready to sink the unwary.

Between the storms, the wind dropped to a manageable 30 knots – almost a Force 7 gale in itself – a relative calm between the storms. To survive these seas we needed to be at our strongest as a team and as individuals. The temptation was to focus just on survival. To 'batten down the hatches' and neglect the wider potential of such a journey, to focus only on the task ahead.

But for our team, this leg was about to become even tougher as we were to lose a crew member before the start. I will spare the finer details, as it is a private story in a public arena. One of my crew, while battling the oceans, had a private battle on her hands with cancer. Determined to take part and be in control of her own destiny, and despite extensive chemotherapy during the training, my crew member fully immersed herself in our race. With an infectious vigour and lust for life, she was the core of our strong team, a focal point for energy and love, a great sailor and a superb role model.

At each port, tests were carried out to monitor the cancer. Two days before we left Buenos Aires the results returned to say that all was not well. She would be forced to leave our yacht and return to the UK for further treatment – we would enter the Southern Ocean a 'man down', an incomplete team, compromised before we began.

Were I or my team to focus purely on the task of racing against the winds and southern seas, perhaps we would have accepted the offer from the race organisers that we take on board a young, fit Argentinian Olympic sailor. But, collectively, that was not even considered. We expected our team member to join us in New Zealand; we wanted nobody to 'fill her berth'; we felt complete even with a distant friend.

The emotions were high as we prepared the yacht, slipped our lines and motored to the start line in the bay. We would have to navigate the tricky waters of the River Plate and the shallow reaches of the Banco Ingles, the shallow bank of treacherous, shifting, unstable mud before the first waves of the southern oceans wet our decks.

As we ventured south, I scribbled three interlocking circles on the side of the navigational chart of the area: those of task, team and individual. This was Adair's Action Centred Leadership model. They seemed small against the expanse of blue on my chart, but they were big in impact. How could I make this toughest of challenges into a growth opportunity? This was a far bigger test than Hurricane Michael.

The elements were not going to let us dwell on our loss for long. Our first night at sea was chaos. A massive katabatic wind hit us. We were slow to react and our mainsail split. For the next 36 days, save for a 'truce' on Christmas Day, there was always a sail on the saloon table being sewn by hand by us all – by the time we reached New Zealand we had completed over 3 kilometres of stitching in tough sailcloth in a pitching, freezing, soaking boat.

Three circles!

I had to ensure that I balanced the needs of 'achieving the task', 'building the team' and 'developing the individuals'. I forced myself not just to focus on the task, but to make sure I did more with it. We did, after all, still have a heck of a long way to go in this race: we were only 8,000 miles down, with 24,000 still to go.

My slightly smaller team were going to have to pull together as one tight-knit unit; I was going to have to ask one hell of a lot from each individual and they would learn about themselves and each other as a result. Any gaps in the team, and the storms would prise it apart. Any failings in the ability of the individuals and the waves would take care of them.

So, with the storm clouds brewing, the seas rising and the wind hitting the boat harder with each gust, I knew that it was not just about these storms: it was about us. We were strong when we tamed Hurricane Michael. We were 'large' when the waves were large. I knew we could do this.

The Southern Ocean presented me with a superb team-building tool and an individual development opportunity, as well as a chance to stamp our mark on the race. Was I crazy?

Revisiting Adair's model

Let's take a closer look at all three aspects of John Adair's powerful thinking.

Achieving the task

What was our task? 'Survive' the Southern Ocean? 'Avoid' the storms? Or 'attack' the challenge? We did not have the time to clearly define our task in the last few whirlwind days in Buenos Aires – there was too much going on and too many conflicting demands. The wider goal was set – reach Wellington – but the specific intent would have to be agreed and committed to by us all.

We discussed what this leg of the race meant to us all. We spoke about our colleague in London and what she would like. The emotions were high but the thinking clear. This leg was for our friend. We wanted her to be proud of us. We wanted her to rejoin us. We agreed to win this leg for her. We would give it our all.

Another big learning here was about who agreed what the task was. I knew what I wanted but I had to 'sell' my wants to the whole team, being cognisant of their motivational needs. I sold it to all, so they could realise their own needs from the task itself. I was able to gain their commitment to the task. They still lived with fear as we approached the storms – so did I, to be honest – but we had chosen a path, we believed in our ability to achieve it, we understood the parameters, we saw our own individual motivational needs within, so were able to commit individually and as a team.

When you set a task, who decides what it is, exactly? How do you sell it to your team? Or do you just 'direct'? Even if a task is set for you by the bigger organisation, is it not your leadership role to ensure you deliver the task to the best of your individual abilities and the abilities of your team? If so, then part of your role is to 'stop before you begin' and sell it to your teams, gain their commitment and ensure they have the competence.

Building the team

How could our predicament become a team-building tool? Southern Ocean, man down! Actually, it was more. I share my thoughts on the difference between team bonding, team building and team development later in this book. I wanted to make sure that we did all three.

Let's quickly look at what does bring a team together. A shared endeavour. Each with a defined role and an understanding of how their efforts contribute to the whole. A deep understanding of the people around them. A meaningful challenge, yet one that is believed to be achievable. Hardship. Direction and support. An external threat. An achievement.

All these aspects of activity will make a team strong.

Developing the individuals

Many within my team shone. They rose to the challenge in ways that I would not have predicted. They displayed huge amounts of personal responsibility; acceptance, not victimhood; reflection, not sorrow; total commitment. Consciously applying John Adair's model helped me ensure that I empowered my team; I was able to let go of more with each mile passing under our keel.

I was hugely motivated to win this leg for my crew, absent and present. I could see how much it meant to them. I would give my all, but for me to be truly effective I had to learn to let go. We would be in the Southern Ocean for a whole month, 24 hours a day – a relentless drive to perform.

I could not be omnipresent; I could not become the 'choke point' for decision making and empowerment. I had to be able to let go. In a business context, this is particularly true. You can lead one task, be the focal point of all decisions and put yourself at the centre. But you cannot do that with two tasks, three or more. You can manage one project, but you need to lead a programme.

How often, when the pressure is on, do you tighten control rather than free it, where you make yourself the indispensable decision maker, the ultimate choke point? One of my pet hates is the new, 'always-on' culture of the permanent accessibility of a leader, which means that even if you are on holiday or on the toilet, you can still call the shots.

What unfolded was at an emotional level I have not encountered before or since. I loved the Southern Ocean. I loved its raw power and beauty, its immensity, the sheer scale. At times we would be more than 1,800 miles from land.

I loved the exquisite nature of the oceans; the mighty albatross effortlessly gliding over the waves, flying nonstop for years, literally; the storm petrel, so small and fragile yet totally at one with the storms and surf; and the skies, enormous, sometimes grey, sometimes a phenomenal display as the aurora australis – or the Southern Lights – blasts your senses. And in our little boat, our island in the seas, I loved it – the rhythms of life at sea, the rituals and the work of sailing itself.

One hugely emotional part of our weekly routines was our Sunday services. No matter the weather, we held a Sunday service in the 'dogs' (the 'dog watches' are two short two-hour shifts around teatime that create an odd number of shifts, hence a change in the shift pattern every day). I am not particularly religious, as you may have guessed by now, but I am hugely spiritual (whatever that may mean for you) and strongly believe in the efficacy of reflection and meditation. I also strongly believe in the power of 'gathering the troops', of creating mechanisms whereby the whole team can gather and be as one.

The Sunday service allowed that to happen in a deep and meaningful way. It also allowed me to feed back to the collective team any concerns or issues, or notes of praise in my 'church notices' part of each service. Using Adair's model, this allowed me to address the 'team' element very effectively. The sick crew member was a devout Catholic and emailed prayers from her hospital bed in London. A crew member would volunteer to read the prayer which, invariably, was a beautifully written and inspiring missive about courage, strength, will, life and love. The spray hid the tears.

There is more to this journey across the bottom of the world than I can tell in this book (it may be something for my next), but we fought hard against the rest of the fleet to work with the wind and waves, so, after over a month at sea and no more than 30 miles to go, we found we had a 12-mile lead over the fleet. We were going to win! Over 6,000 miles and 36 days of non-stop effort and our win for our absent crew member, our manifestation of solidarity and support was about to be fulfilled. Only 30 miles to go – 4 hours max – and we were 12 miles, almost 2 hours, ahead of the next yacht.

I have learned much on my journey in life, but no lesson was as hard as this. With the trophy almost in my hands, disaster struck. A massive storm that had been brewing deep in the Tasmanian Sea hit the shallows of the Cook Straits – which separate the North and South Islands of New Zealand – with impeccably bad timing. As we entered the mountainous funnel of the approaches to 'windy Wellington', and as the seas shallowed at the edge of the continental shelf from being 4,000 metres deep to a mere 40 metres, we were hit by massive winds.

The narrator in the documentary of our race tells of 'the worst seas of the leg', but he was wrong. These were the worst seas I have ever encountered in all my years of sailing. Hurricane Michael was child's play by comparison. With the wind gusting to 70 knots (not forecast), and with the seas tripping over themselves presenting rolling breakers, our foresail exploded as we peaked one of these mighty crests; the strain was too much. With a crack like that of a pistol shot, the sail disintegrated. Flailing canvas caught in the rigging. The noise was incredible. The whole yacht was shaking itself to pieces as every new gust flogged the sail and us further. With the sail stuck in the rigging, we lost all power. Now entirely at the mercy of the seas, we battled for over an hour, the mast frequently dipping into the water, to bring this beast under control. Counting the crew, preserving life, taming the sail and all the time slipping back away from Wellington. We had to keep calm, keep alive, but we needed control – and quickly.

As quickly as the winds had come, so they dropped. Not to

a calm but just to a storm. The second-placed boat, still in the calmer, deeper waters, could see our troubles. Its crew saw our sail explode, saw us being swept away by each breaking wave. One of the disadvantages of being in the lead is that you provide a signal to the rest on the good and the bad. The second-placed boat, skippered by Conrad Humphreys, a brilliant young sailor, tucked in under the cliffs, out of the wind, and snatched the lead.

All our efforts were to no avail. We recovered the yacht before losing another place and limped into Wellington in second place. A quiet, subdued crew doused the sails after 36 days of Southern Ocean might, a glazed and tired look deep in their eyes. A win for our suffering crew was now gone.

But what put it all into perspective was that, as the ropes were thrown ashore, suddenly from out of the crowd we saw our friend. She was back. We were complete again. The tears of sorrow of Buenos Aires were washed away with the tears of joy.

(Just to let you know, we completed our race around the world as a 'complete crew' and the battle for life was won. And you can read about how we battled Hurricane Michael in Chapter 6.)

That leg of our race, Leg 3, the first of two Southern Ocean legs, was an extraordinary time. There are enough stories in that one leg for a book, a film and a conference. Another time!

Every day of that leg, on the side of the chart and in the front of my mind, steering all my actions, were the three interlocking circles created by John Adair.

We grew stronger as a team and many of the crew members found new strengths and capabilities within. Mission accomplished. Task achieved. Team built. Individuals developed. Check! That was more than just surviving a threat: it was maximising an opportunity. The return on my 'balanced-leadership investment' paid dividends over and over again as the race unfolded.

Imagine what could have been had I not applied the principles of task, team andindividual. Would we have come through the Southern Ocean in first – aargh, second! – place with a team not fully committed to the task? Would the team be stronger as a result so that, when we arrived back in Southampton after 32,000 miles and 9 months, we'd be the only boat in the whole fleet not to have crew members leave before setting sail? We started with a total team of 27 and finished with 27 – I was very proud of that.

And would the people within my team have grown in stature and confidence to such a degree that, years later, while joining me for coffee, one of my team – the one we called 'the Professor' (about whom more later) – would remark, 'You know, Skipper, I'm still the same person, I live in the same house, go to the same coffee house; I'm still me – but the difference is, I walk taller'?

I doubt it!

So, to paraphrase Abraham Lincoln, why go to work chopping that tree with a blunt axe? Sure, with hard work, big effort and loads of time, you'll get there. But how about we have leadership presence and leadership courage so that, before we go hitting that tree, we spend some good time making sure that we are properly equipped to do it well and to the best of our, and our team's, ability with a sharp axe? How about we lead in a compassionate way?

I say, 'Give me a strong and cohesive team of developed and committed individuals and I will achieve any and every task you give me.'

Over to you!

Changing your attitude

An attitude to adopt in any situation is not that of just 'Can I do it?' It's also that of reflecting and asking:

- Can my team do it?
- What can I learn?
- What can my team learn?

- How can I use this to build my team for more and bigger tasks later down the line?
- Who within my team can use this as an opportunity to build and help on their life's journey?
- How can I use this to empower my team and get them to own it?
- How can I use this to let go, create a legacy and move ever onwards and upwards?

In other words, be a Compassionate Leader, look ahead, grow your people and be able to achieve more as a result.

All of my work is actually centred on Adair's model of balancing the needs. This book revolves around it. My work on creating whole-scale cultural change is driven by the model, and, whenever I coach or work with leaders across all business fields, I am working towards creating the understanding that, for long-term, sustainable high performance, the leader will need to balance their efforts between 'achieving the task', 'building the team' and 'developing the individuals'. Thank you, John Adair!

A closer look at Adair's model

I apply John Adair's thinking at home, when I am coaching rugby or sailing, and most certainly when I am working with a team in one of my expeditions. It informs the design of all my work. For the last 30-odd years, subconsciously and lately more consciously, I have adopted the principles therein.

So let's look more closely at Adair's model of Action Centred Leadership.

I must advise you here that I am not pretending to be an expert. I am sharing with you my interpretation and application of all that I have learned. You can and should reference his work directly at the official website (johnadair.co.uk) – there is much more to find there.

I access the model in a number of ways. Before an executive

board can effectively create or work to a strategic intent, it needs to be able to work closely together as a team. Before it can become a team, the individuals within need to raise their own self-awareness to be able to relate more effectively with others.

If an organisation needs to change course, either through voluntary intent or enforced external demands, it will need to define where the new direction is and what new behaviours will deliver that strategic intent, build the team to do so and gain the commitment from the individuals.

Before any team within an organisation can align and commit to a strategic endeavour, a task or a culture, they must be a strong team first. And, before that can happen, the rules of the Me, You and Us model need to be applied.

Before a leader can effectively task a team to tackle a particular activity, there is work to be done in ensuring the team can work together effectively and that the right people are within the team to do what needs to be done.

In my life as an occasional expedition leader I need to consider the following:

- THE TASK: What am I hoping to do and why? Have I gained the commitment of the people within my team? Planning? Logistics? Training? Media?
- THE TEAM: Are we all on board? Do we have the complementary skills required? Have we all bought into the why and how? Do we have a common culture and a strong understanding and commitment to it? Do my team members all 'know' each other?
- THE INDIVIDUALS: Do I have the right people? Do I know them? How will this help them in their life's journey? What extra skills do they need? Are all the roles and responsibilities mapped and agreed? Secondary roles too?

When we looked at the question of balancing needs earlier in this chapter, I introduced the example of fixing the shed. As a father, rather than just push on and 'fix the shed', I decided that this could give me an opportunity to, well, be a father. So let's stick with the shed awhile.

The task

The shed needs fixing (and there are a million other things that need doing, too). This is the **task**. Have I got the right tools and so forth?

The team

But hang on a second. It isn't just me. What about Frey and Arabella, my children – the **team**? This job might take a bit longer with them, but then they will learn and maybe do the next job. As a team we can do more. And I love them and want to spend time with them. And I want them to understand that they need to 'chip in', too, with the family effort. It will take longer but it will be more fun for sure (possibly more frustrating, too, if I have the wrong attitude).

The individuals

This is a great opportunity for them as **individuals** to learn how to do things, how to hammer a nail, saw wood, screw a screw. They will also learn about teamwork and family responsibility. It will be a great lesson in the joy of giving and the value of teamwork. It will develop their self-worth. It will, eventually, help them do what I know they must: fly the nest.

Opportunities to do more

See how much more you can achieve by applying this philosophy?

Any task is now an opportunity to do more later. Remember:

true control comes from letting go. You cannot grow or take on more unless you grow the people around you to support you. You cannot multitask unless you can trust and empower your team. You cannot move on and leave a vacuum behind – this is about legacy.

Don't be busy, be busy being smart. Remember the sharp axe!

In other words, this model is right in line with my thinking on what Compassionate Leadership is all about.

The model explains the three areas of focus that every leader, parent, friend or colleague needs to be cognisant of and active in. Divide your attention equally into responsibility for achieving the task, responsibility for the team and responsibility for each individual. To lose sight of these three interrelated areas will cause imbalance and, ultimately, loss of credibility with the individuals and team and loss of success in achieving the task.

Over a period of time, monitor which circle you are spending your time in. It may be that, if you redraw the circles relative in size to how much time you spend focusing on each area, you will have one big 'task' circle and the other two of 'team' and 'individual' lost in the shadow.

Go on – draw the circles, monitor your focus every day, every week, over a quarter; create a long-term balance.

And, when you hear people say, 'I'm a task-focused kind of guy' and they think they are being clever, well, you know the reality! At what cost, and how effectively? Who wants a blunt axe?

A final word on balance

Before we leave the idea of balance in leadership, here is a thought to challenge accepted wisdom and cultures that would have a massive impact on creating a long-term, sustainable, high-performance organisation. It feeds into the Me, You and Us model and aligns with all three areas of John Adair's superb model of Action Centred Leadership. It taps into building people's capabilities as well as their engagement. It encourages activity, challenge, development and the principle of continuous improvement. It is a big part of fulfilling self-worth!

Let's celebrate failure!

'What?' I hear you ask. *'Loser!'* Or words to that effect.

But I don't mean failure through lack of effort or gross misconduct. I mean failure when the intent was pure and the effort high. I mean 'committed failure'.

We celebrate success, of course. That's when we have won something, achieved something. When we have hit a milestone, made a delivery, got the key performance indicator ticked, crossed the line. It is good to celebrate success. It spurs us on for more success. It taps into our motivation to succeed. It drives more delivery and greater success. We learn why we succeeded so we can do it again. Sell more. Grow. Get bigger.

But you know what? Yes and no! We need a balance.

Think about the Three Needs Theory we encountered in Chapter 6. Look at the Me, You and Us thinking. Remind yourself of the need for self-worth that drives us all. How are you going to encourage crazy ideas, the 20/24 thinking you'll read about in Chapter 10 that enabled winning the race to the Magnetic North Pole? Don't forget the power of gaining commitment rather than just forcing compliance. What lessons are you actually reinforcing in your team's brains? What power base do you want to be given?

If I celebrate only success, I am tapping into just a third of people's motivational needs and potentially motivating only a third of my team, thus losing commitment and disabling fulfilment and feelings of self-worth.

This has the effect of potentially closing down people's admission when things go wrong, because they will hide errors. It reinforces the fear of failure.

By creating a 'morgue' around failure I do not encourage learning. If we learn by failure – and I very strongly believe we do – then, unless people feel they can fail, they won't try.

If I also celebrate 'committed failure', I am:

- recognising effort and rewarding it, thus creating a culture of 'effort and pure intent'
- tapping into everybody's motivational needs, thus gaining commitment and enabling self-worth
- encouraging innovation and the willingness to try – 20/24 (see Chapter 10)
- allowing 'quick failure' and refocusing of efforts to new ideas

Create a 'learning' culture

We need to balance the needs of task, team and individual. So let us celebrate 'success' *and* 'committed failure'.

Consider the work that your teams are applying themselves to now. Consider what 'celebrations' you have had in the past. What opportunities exist to 'celebrate committed failure'?

How many times did Edison fail in discovering the electric light? Or did he just discover 10,000 ways that it would not work and at each new 'discovery' get closer and closer to his goal? Albert Einstein said that a person who never made a mistake never tried anything new.

How many hurdles did the gold-medal-winning Olympic hurdler knock over on their path to glory? Ten thousand? A hundred thousand? How many of those were 'failures' – or how many were put down to effort and the desire to succeed? It is when you stop knocking them over that learning stops!

Rudyard Kipling beautifully captures the reality around success and failure by calling them both 'impostors' in his beautiful and incredibly perceptive poem 'If', which I strongly recommend to all leaders: 'If you can meet with Triumph and Disaster / And treat those two impostors just the same ...'

Yes, it's about balance.

Key learnings

- Compassionate Leadership is about legacy, longevity, performance and people.

- John Adair's superb leadership model shows we need to balance our time between achieving the task, building the team and developing the individual.

- Let us celebrate honest failure and recognise effort and intent.

- Why try to chop down a tree with a blunt axe – have the courage to stop and sharpen your axe.

EXERCISE: BALANCING TIME AND FOCUS

The temptation is that we focus only on delivering the task and not on building the team or developing the individuals within. Hacking away at the tree with a blunt axe.

Map your time in a day, a week and over a month. Redraw Adair's three circles in relative size to the time you spend in each, then create an action plan to rebalance to three *equal* circles. Here's a grid that might help.

Activity	Focus	Action plan
Board meeting	Mainly on delivery items, nothing on developing people, and no effort on team.	Consider including a 'social' element to build relationships. Put 'development' as the first item on the agenda.

EXERCISE: CELEBRATIONS!

Consider the work that your teams are applying themselves to now. Consider what 'celebrations' you have had in the past. What opportunities exist to 'celebrate committed failure'?

Notes

_____

_____

_____

_____

_____

_____

_____

_____

_____

_____

_____

_____

_____

CHAPTER 9

CULTURE CLARITY

Coming together is a beginning. Keeping together is progress. Working together is success.

– Henry Ford

There is so much written about the importance of an established culture in an organisation. Culture eats strategy for breakfast, apparently. The time to create a culture that drives high performance is not when you are in the thick of it, but before you set sail. A high-performance culture needs to be embedded before the battle commences. Leave it too late and your fight will be significantly harder.

When the seas are calm, the culture of your teams and organisation will probably survive scrutiny. The luxury of time and choice affords you space to enjoy the positive aspects of a winning team and all the spoils that brings. When the pressure is off, you could get away without having a defined and agreed culture. Yet leaving the creation of your culture until you're out on the high seas will leave you sinking beneath the water.

In times of threat, high pressure and stress, ambiguity of what is expected of you in terms of behaviour or role will only increase indecision and doubt. It is easy to 'intellectually agree' to behave in a certain way when the stakes are low, but to 'emotionally agree', to commit, to a certain way in tough times, well, that cannot happen lightly. However, it is when the expectations are high and the external variables are stressing the system that we need everyone to behave in an understood way, a way that maintains the drive to deliver strategy, and not in a way that is focused purely on self-preservation.

Take a moment to think how this could impact on your organisation. If your teams lost focus on delivery just when it was needed, how would this affect your performance? At exactly the time when not to succeed means to fail – completely – your teams start falling apart, tensions rise, communication fails and emotions run high. Uncertainty over how to react in a pressured environment could multiply exponentially at just the time when you need to rely on your team to be motivated, loyal and committed. In this situation a 'victim' mentality can rapidly develop, blame rises, collaboration drops and our 'primitive' (or 'lizard') brain kicks in when, in reality, our survival demands greater cooperation and understanding, not less.

In my experience of working with businesses and sporting teams, where they take culture seriously and consider 'cultural fit' to be the first element of recruitment and performance, they excel. I like my rugby, as you know, and I like the way the New Zealand All Blacks have created a phenomenally strong team culture. And the results follow! And I like how Stuart Lancaster, who became the England rugby coach in 2012, enabled a meteoric transformation of the whole of English rugby through an emphasis of 'culture first' – his inspiration coming from the remarkable and hugely successful philosophies of Bill Walsh, the head coach for the San Francisco 49ers, and articulated in his excellent book *The Score Takes Care of Itself* – I cannot recommend this enough. (Reflecting on the closing of the last chapter, when we discussed celebrating honest failure, Bill Walsh once said to his team during a half-time talk when the scoreboard showed they were being handsomely beaten, 'I don't care if you lose, it is how you lose that matters'. The turnaround in the second half was dramatic!) The team at Mission

Performance spent much time and effort focusing on developing cultures, and I learned much from them. Thank you!

Understanding culture

Let's begin with understanding what culture actually is.

The Oxford English dictionary describes culture as 'the attitudes and behaviour characteristics of a particular social group'. In other words;

- 'It's the way we do things around here.'
- 'It's our collective way of doing things.'
- 'It's the way we behave.'

A key understanding when we talk about culture is that culture is defined by a 'collective behaviour'. Whereas individuals have their own separate behaviours and values, if we come together and agree to behave in a certain way, and those behaviours support an agreed set of values, that then becomes the culture. So a culture is having an agreed set of behaviours and values to help us when times are tough and when times are good.

And a culture is so much more than just an internal behavioural framework: it also defines you to the outside world; it sets expectations for all stakeholders; and it impacts on perceptions as well as relationships.

Clarity

The first characteristic of a high-performance culture is its clarity. By this I mean a clear direction in terms of:

- What we are doing and where we are going?
- How we are doing it?
- Why we are doing it?

Clarity and the setting of the strategic intent are important: we need to know where we are going and what we are doing. But it is more than just the 'what' and the 'where'. To be truly meaningful and to be able to gain a commitment to the cause, you need to define the 'why' and embed this way before 'setting sail' – organisations that can define the 'why' accelerate. The philosopher Friedrich Nietzsche understood this well when he said, 'He who has a why to live can bear almost any how'!

Both individuals and teams must have a clear understanding of where they are going and understand how their contributions support the central purpose of the endeavour. When there is clarity within a team there is transparency of roles, expectations and processes as well as honest, open communication to allow discussions over conflict handling and resolution, fears, anxieties, strengths and weaknesses.

Character

We do what we do because of who we are. It's quite simple. When we approach a task or interact with a person, so much of what we do is automatically programmed within us. We behave as we do because it has worked for us so far, because it fits with our own values and motivations, and because it doesn't contradict our belief systems. We all go to work to do our best, to do 'the right thing' according to what we *believe* is 'the right thing'. 'The right thing' isn't something we decide on every moment and with every interaction, but is something that has been built up within us through our experiences and based on the values instilled into us as children.

It is this 'character' that defines our actions, both as individuals and as teams. It is this 'character' that drives our performance. This combination of values, beliefs and experiences within each individual is multiplied by each team member and this, in turn, comprises the 'culture', and ultimately the performance, of a team.

So, individually we have a particular character, and collectively it is a culture. The words, essentially, are interchangeable. When you think of the *character* of a group, it has the same meaning as the word *culture* in this context. In order for the performance of a team to be high, the culture must be one that encourages the development of the individual, according to their character. This requires recognising and rewarding the 'right' behaviours and discouraging those behaviours that are 'wrong' and do not contribute to the team and organisation as a whole.

Individual characters make up a team character. Team characters make up an organisational culture.

But it is not quite as simple as saying that an individual's character can change when they are threatened or in conflict. In order to fully understand the culture of your organisation, you need to understand not only what happens when the sea is smooth, but also what happens when you're riding choppy waters. Causes of potential conflict must be understood and addressed, and individuals and teams need to be able to understand and buy into the organisational culture and purpose to fully engage and exhibit commitment as opposed to compliance.

This reinforces the 'knowing you' element of emotional intelligence expected of a Compassionate Leader – not just their strengths and weaknesses, but what motivates your people, how they are affected by pressure and change, what their conflict triggers may be.

Identity

The third part of the equation is that of identity. We are essentially a tribal species. A sense of belonging is core to fulfilment for human beings. What we identify with and refer to is really key to us. Even on a very small island such as Britain, people get very excited about the difference between North and South, county versus county, one side of the street and the other. In

London, they distinguish between north and south of the river. Try getting a taxi to cross the water! We have our religious cultures, our language, our sports teams whom we relate to and passionately follow. Imagine a Venn diagram with all these interlocking identities and a bit in the middle that is the common element – our individual identity. So, for a team to come together and to work together strongly as a unit, understanding that identity is essential.

When a team are clear about what they do, and agreed on how they will behave in order to do it, they have a clear identity – a 'brand', if you like, something that each member is enthused and inspired by. It is important that this 'identity' be interdependent, otherwise you merely have a collection of individuals. When added to clarity and character, identity is what leads to the team coming together and generating commitment. It delivers the basic human need to connect.

Let me share with you an example of how all these elements have worked for me. As we saw earlier, when sailing around the world in the BT Global Challenge, we became known as Team Large, and there's a lovely story behind it.

I recall the night I first met my Global Challenge team. They came from all walks of life, from all over the world. Within my boat there were people of all levels of experience and expectation. Eight had never sailed before. A few had at a good competitive level. We had 'fair-weather' sailors and we had a couple of strong offshore veterans. A mix not unlike any other team in the world. How often are you given the opportunity to create a team from scratch, given a blank sheet of paper and freedom to select whomsoever you wish? Pretty rare, huh? Invariably, the teams you inherited would not be unlike mine on board our yacht.

Sir Charles Blyth (better known as Chay Blyth, the Scotsman who, in 1971, was the first person to sail westwards around the world single-handed and nonstop) was the organiser of the race. He was a man of theatre. He had arranged to use one of the large conference suites at the Earls Court Boat Show to announce the teams. All the crew volunteers for the race, some 300 people, came together in a large room with a large screen and stage. Chay was on the stage sharing salty stories of derring-do and adventure.

The 12 skippers were dotted around the sides of the room. Each skipper had a large banner proclaiming their team name. At this time most of the skippers had sponsors, so we had Team Compaq, Team Norwich Union, Team Logica and so on; and then there were a couple of the skippers who didn't have sponsors. I was one of them and my banner just said TEAM HOPKINSON. I looked at this amazing sea of excited faces and I had no idea who was going to sail with me; likewise, they didn't know whom they were going to sail with. They didn't know who their team mates were going to be, who their sponsor was or who their skipper was.

Chay Blyth, having raised the levels of excitement and apprehension to the same level, then announced the teams. There were cheers, gasps, screams of delight and groans of horror! It was an exciting time for everybody and, as the final team was announced, he said, 'Right, aff ye goo' in his thick Scottish accent. From that incredible confusion came order. Suddenly, I noticed among the sea of faces that some of them were looking intently at me.

When I look back and tell the story it still sends tingles down my spine for it was then, and only then, that I realised the responsibility that I was taking on board as a skipper in this incredible race. All these people had made an investment in their lives. An investment and trust in their skipper. They had made an investment in me. They had put their own lives and dreams in my hands. And this is true in any form of leadership: that people make an investment in you. I realised that night that it was my job, before, during and after the race, to give them a return on their investment. How awful it would be if they invested all that time, money and effort and I gave them nothing back! A Compassionate Leader always considers the 'return' on the investment made in them.

Now there were 12 distinct groups of people, each group surrounding a team placard. The noise was incredible. Regardless of modesty and propriety, teams stripped off their shirts to don their new sponsor shirts. Now there were distinct splashes of colour around the room starting to define the teams. The race organisers had given the skippers with no sponsor brightly coloured rugby shirts to help with the formation of a team identity. Ours were a rather horrible purple colour. In retrospect, I might well have invested in sorting my own out.

A very good team-building tool, when used at the right time and in the right quantity, is a small libation. If you take nothing else away from this book, take that one!

'Come on, team, follow me,' I bellowed across the din. 'To the pub. Hurrah!'

A chorus of cheers from my team gave me confidence in that they agreed with my first decision.

Here's a part of the story I rarely tell, but I can trust you to keep quiet, can't I? Having spoken to the landlord of the pub the night before to prepare him for the arrival the next night of some 20 very excited and noisy people, I had returned to my hotel room to prepare for the next day. And so it was, as we left Earls Court that night, as I led my team for the very first time in this incredible life-changing voyage, as they put their lives in my hands, I lost my way! Seriously. I could not find the pub. In my defence I had not walked the route from Earls Court to the pub before. It was Danno, the policeman in the team, who first noticed. 'Erm, do you know where you're going, Skipper?' Fortunately, he had an A–Z on him and we found our way. I put it down as a deliberate team-building tool as the thinking would now be within the team that they would have to be strong to take this buffoon of a skipper round the world! Quick lesson there about how, as they used to say in the navy, 'prior preparation prevents piss-poor performance'.

Anyway, at last, we found our pub. The landlord had been true to his word. We had an area cordoned off. On the table were bottles of beer and wine, crisps, nuts and pizzas. It was to be one long, loud night.

It was then that they introduced themselves to me, and they introduced themselves in so many different ways. One chap, who became known as Trout, a confident young man, thrust his hand to take mine, looked me in the eye and said, 'I'm here to win. If I'm not in the winning boat I'm out of here now.'

Wow! No pressure, then! He was very competitive, a really nice fellow and a very good sailor. 'Come on in, grab a beer. We'll have plenty of time to set our goals,' came my diplomatic reply.

An older gentleman came forward. 'I'm not sure I can do this, Skipper. I'm an old man. I've never done anything as physical as this. I think I may be a burden on the team.' This is the chap who was nicknamed 'the Professor'. 'Come on board, Professor. You're one of the team. You'll be fine.' As it happened, the Professor was a rock and a mentor to me. He would have been called a 'fair-weather sailor', but not now! Frequently we had chats in the sail locker as I was able to share some of my burden. He was almost always one of the first to notice if I needed help.

Some other members of the team weren't quite sure why they were there. As we introduced ourselves, I asked each the same questions: 'Why are you here?' 'What do you want?' Back came the answers: 'To win.' 'To escape.' 'To change.' And, for many, 'I'm not sure.' Another one, 'Bones', the newly qualified doctor, wanted to understand more about who she was and how other people are; a mixture of a professional development period (imagine a doctor who can relate to their patients) and a chance to do something special before embarking on her full career.

And there was another who used to work at Sainsbury's in Macclesfield (we nicknamed him 'Tesco'). He said he wanted to change his life. Fair call. (No room in this book for this, but I tell Tesco's story a great deal, especially to youth and school groups; it is all about reaching out and making your own life happen.)

It became clear that all the people were on board for completely different reasons and all had massively different expectations, experiences and motivations. How was I going to create a team? What was going to become the catalyst for our union? To be honest, I struggled. How on earth was I going to bring all these diverse people together?

This is true of any team. There is no such thing as a non-diverse group of two or more people. An expression I like to use is that, for everyone in a given room, 'their journey from birth to that room is utterly unique'. So how do you bring them together? How do you help them fulfil their own goals and commit to a combined endeavour?

What was it that was going to allow us to start feeling as one team, to start this whole concept of gelling and coming together?

I had a moment of inspiration after a couple of beers that night (life's like that sometimes!). 'Of course!' I said. 'Identity!' It became clear that we would need to develop our clarity and culture, and we would make time for that, but tonight it was all about creating our identity. Our team name. We didn't have a team name, just 'Team Hopkinson'. We had to create a team name that would be meaningful to us and form the basis of an identity we could all rally behind, an identity we could eventually put words to, put a vision to, put values to, so everyone in the world could know what this team stood for.

After yet another ale, I had another flash of inspiration.

'Gather round, team,' I said. 'I've got a story to tell you.' (As you know, I believe in the power of stories.)

I took them back to the 1991 Rugby World Cup quarterfinal, France versus England, to be played in France. All that season the French forwards had been absolutely magnificent. But so had the English. One of the English forwards came from the 'old school' of rugby, a big chap called Mickey Skinner. Mickey's a great big bear of a man with long red hair. He would never take a step backwards when playing for England. He was interviewed the day before the game and the interviewer said to him, 'So, Mickey, what's it going to be like for you in Paris tomorrow?'

Mickey just leaned into the camera and said, '*Laarrge!*'

And that was it.

It was an amazing game of rugby. I was actually there. France were ahead. It was the final quarter of the game. They were camped on the English line, attack after attack after attack. One more score for France and it would be curtains and death for England. All you could hear were the French crowds baying for English blood.

And then something remarkable happened.

Mickey Skinner pulled off a tackle that became known as the 'hit of the century', in which the French back row peeled off a scrum to a certain score with only one person in their way. Mickey. He went in with such conviction and ferocity that it fundamentally changed the shape of the game. He was so totally committed to saving his line and saving his team that suddenly there was a new belief. The ball spilled from that tackle; England cleared their line. Outnumbered 10–1, the English in the crowd could now be heard screaming their team on. On and off the pitch there was a new sense of resolution; something had shifted. England then fought their way up the pitch and scored in the dying seconds and went on to win that game 19 points to 10.

I told that story to my team (obviously much embellished, as you can imagine). I said, 'Look, team, this is going to be a large race. The winds are going to be large. The waves are going to be large. What I need from you all, at any particular moment, is for us all to dig deep into our inner resolve to come up with moments of largeness like Mickey Skinner.'

So, from that moment on, we were known as Team Large. Everything we did, we gave it large. We were also known as the

Large Ones. Our whole way of life became large. 'Make mine a large one, please, landlord!'

That night was special. Team Large, the 'Large Ones', were born. The short-lived Team Hopkinson had been replaced by something truly special. Throughout the TV coverage of the race the narrative repeated the refrain of 'that most popular of crews, Team Large . . . '

We were different. I was so very proud of the fact that we were the only team with an identity outside the sponsors. When our sponsor, Olympic Group, did come aboard, they were very happy for us to be 'Team Large on Olympic'. So identity was a really key element for us. Thank you, Angelos (the CEO of Olympic Group), for your understanding and your support – it was a very important part of our journey!

Figure 9.1 Team Large

More on clarity

A few days later we looked at what would be behind 'Team Large' – the 'why' and the 'how'. Easy to say, but hard to live. We looked at who we were, what our culture was to be. We discussed what we wanted to achieve and why and what our team clarity statement should be. This is so important to get right, as I explain in other parts of this book. We spent a lot of time thinking, talking, reviewing. Some wanted to win, others to survive or create lifelong friendships. Our inner motivations were bubbling up to the surface. It was clear from a race of this scale and length, with so many variables outside of our control, and with such a diverse crew, that our clarity statement would have to be a hell of a lot more than just about winning. We had to try to create a collective clarity that we could all buy into. This was the first time I used the sticky-note procedure – as we did in the exercise 'The Big Journey' in Chapter 5 – to allow everyone an equal and uninfluenced voice. It turned out to be a life-changing way of creating a cohesive and committed crew.

TO CONTINUOUSLY BUILD, DEVELOP AND SUPPORT EACH OTHER, AS A TEAM, TO ACHIEVE OUR MAXIMUM AND ENJOY OUR CHALLENGE

Figure 9.2 Our team clarity statement

Everyone felt they could be part of this. When Tesco looked at it, to him it was about changing his life. To the Professor, it was about supporting each other. To Trout, it was about achieving our maximum.

Being Team Large, naturally our focus fell onto the word *Maximise* and so we developed our shorthand expression of our team clarity statement:

'Maximise
Speed, Safety, Happiness and Passion'.

In that specific order. Remember that order!

We also came up with some shorter, more attainable goals, which included things such as 'being the first boat into the next port'; 'having the smallest dropout rate in the race'. These were key, but we kept our main goal broad and applicable across the board, as it has been proved that, if your main goal is too specific, it can demotivate. Give it a range, a breadth, and it will inspire and stretch but not frighten!

Culture

We then spent a great deal of time discussing how to 'live large', how to deliver on that clarity, what it meant to be Team Large – our character or culture.

The output of the exercise involving the sticky notes informed this as well (see Big Journey exercise on pp. 70–75). When you look at the notes people make about the environment they want to work in, focus on the synergies, match them to the clarity, it becomes clear that culture cannot be imposed, but grows organically.

Your role as a leader in this process is to steer and guide. Be careful of 'telling', or else the emotional buy-in and ownership from your crew will be weakened. If what you want does not 'appear', then introduce it, suggest it. For example, on a boat, punctuality is so important, so I introduced the topic and let the team decide the rule.

If I make up the rules, I have to be the policeman. If I force the culture, I have to supervise the compliant reactions. But, if my team create them, my team decide, and I just guide and advise, then they 'own' the culture, they become the policemen of their own standards. If I say, 'We must be on time,' I will have to be master of the clock, and so not be able to fulfil my role as leader.

We chose not to use standard values-type words, but to make phrases and statements of our own. They had meaning to us. Behind each statement were notes capturing what it meant, what 'acts' and 'behaviours' would make it real. For example, for punctuality, my team came up with 'on time all the time'.

This is another absolutely vital understanding for setting a culture. It is not enough to have 'words stuck on a wall': they need to be translated in to real-life actions – actions that people can perform and others can see. As the great Aristotle once said, 'We are what we repeatedly do; excellence, therefore, is not an act, but a habit.' Our 'on time all the time' definition of punctuality made the action of '10 minutes early is late' specific, measurable, doable and owned by the team.

See it

Do it

Do it well

Deal with it and let it go

Push the limit

Lean on me

Be true

Respect

On time all the time

Large laughs

Out of the box

Stop learning

Stop breathing

Figure 9.3 The Team Large culture

We spoke of topics like 'support', 'performance' 'arguments' and 'love'!

Love was a tricky one to put on the table, but it had to be done. Imagine someone falling in love with another mid-ocean. They would want to be with each other, gazing into each other's eyes, distracted from the job in hand. Then they might fall out – jealousy, envy, heavy emotions, mid-ocean! A recipe for disaster! I had to discourage love affairs on board. So how do you introduce that one? 'OK, team, one more to agree on. You can only start going out with each other once you've gone out with the rest of the fleet first. Discuss.' It worked! I think two of my crew took me up on the challenge.

The test

Let me move forward many months now, when we started to approach our first storm near an area of the North Atlantic called the Flemish Cap just before the Grand Banks. (A few weeks before we set sail, the film *The Perfect Storm* hit the shores of England. I tried to ban the crew from watching George Clooney battling the mighty oceans and almost dying in the process, but to no avail – the crew went as one.) As we approached our first test as a team, a big storm in a notoriously vicious sea, I was thinking, This is the chance to see if our culture stands the test – here we go!

This, our first storm, was going to be a big one, but we approached it with optimism – potentially blind optimism. *How* we approached it was going to impact on the rest of our race: if we were too cautious, we'd drop back; if we were too aggressive, we could be hurt.

We decided to go for speed. We wanted to set the attitude right at the beginning of the race, as much a statement to ourselves as it was for the other 11 yachts. We've already seen how we had to fight our way through Hurricane Michael, how we decided to 'attack' it. That could happen only as a result of our actions with our first storm, and these actions were driven not by experience, for we had none as this crew, but by our culture and our clarity.

You'll remember the definition of our clarity when shone through the prism of our culture, our values. We had created the desire to maximise. Remember the order of the words? *Speed,* followed by *safety,* then *happiness* and *passion.*

We were able to be aggressive and confident with our first storm only because our clarity and character had put the word *speed* before the word *safety.* Another boat in the same race had those two words the other way around and they were not given permission by themselves to actually attack the storms. By their own words, they had put safety first and it would have gone contrary to their collective value set, their culture. One decision, two words, yet a world of difference. In fact, after the storm had passed, that particular boat ended up three days behind the fleet. So having that vision and those values, having that clarity, having that character that supported our identity was so important.

So, as you embark on creating a strong and coherent culture, be very careful what you create, for it will give you permission and will also stop you from acting in particular ways. It is not an exercise to take lightly. It will drive commitment to your cause, and it will also deny you other actions that are contrary to your 'clarity'.

When we are in a tough space, we tend to fall back on our own protection mechanisms. I have my own character and my own way of looking after myself, as do we all. That will not help, though, in a team context, because what happens under stress is that the team falls apart. But if a team has a collective character – a culture, in other words, so that we know how we need to behave – then that's what we fall back on. We understand how each team member is going to behave and what we're going to do.

So, when it came to storms and hurricanes, we knew what to expect of each other and what was expected of ourselves. We knew that our clarity and culture had enabled us, given us permission, to attack the storm. I'm very happy to say that when the waves died down we came out of that storm, and later Hurricane Michael, in first place. When the seas got large, we got large. It was all in the name.

I cannot stress enough how important it is to put the work in before the battle, when the pressure is not on. Put the work in, and get it right. Sharpen that axe! This will support you in the good times and save you in the bad, and ensure that the right decisions are made for your teams, regardless of the severity of challenge. And, if you're reading this and saying, 'I'm already at action stations, it's too late to start,' you are wrong. Stop. You cannot afford not to. Do it now, before you get in deeper. Have the courage we spoke about earlier, that 'leadership courage' to stop, define the clarity and culture, ensure everyone can rally behind the identity and then resume. It will pay dividends; it may even mean survival.

A short story to bring it alive. I have mentioned one of my heroes, Admiral Horatio Nelson, before (there is so much you can learn from a man like that). In the Battle of Trafalgar, over 200 years ago, Britain was going to take on the combined fleets of France and Spain. Britain had 27 warships; they had 33. Their ships were bigger than ours. The British were heavily outnumbered in guns, too. It was to be a crucial battle for all the countries involved. This was one of the turning points of the histories of the nations and their empires. Whichever nation won this particular battle was going to have the freedom of the seas, and at that time this meant the freedom of the routes of communication and trade all around the world. So you could argue that was exactly the time that really strong leadership was needed.

'Thank goodness we had an excellent leader like Nelson in charge!' I hear you say. As it happened, the French were wise to that, too, and a marksman shot him in the first 20 minutes. He died in the first few hours and had no direct impact on the battle itself. Yet, as history will tell us, it was a resounding success for Britain.

So why was it that it didn't matter that the leader wasn't there? This is such a great story on what leadership is really about, and about clarity and culture. It was what Nelson did *before* the battle that counted. Over the years he had got to know his captains well. As a fleet, they had been engaged with the enemy in running a 'global blockade' for some two years. There was a lot of experience and knowledge, and it would have been easy to argue that nothing extra was needed before engaging in a full-blown sea battle. But Nelson thought otherwise. He knew how important this was to be. Extra investment was needed before it got 'too hot', as he used to say.

As he assembled the fleet, he invited all the captains into his cabin on HMS *Victory*. What he did not do was to 'tell' them what to do. This was no directive. First, he painted in their minds a vision of what the world would look like after they won the Battle of Trafalgar, how the British ships would have the freedom of the seas, how Britain would be able to trade as she wished, how her language would be the *lingua franca*. The Empire could grow and their families would be safe back home. He established the 'why' – the purpose and real meaning behind the battle.

He then brought them back to the aftermath of the battle and conjured the mental image of the sinking and burning French and Spanish ships, and the British fleet still afloat. Then he asked them to share. 'You were with me at the Nile, what happened there?' 'Remember Copenhagen? What can we take from that battle and apply to this?' He allowed each captain to share his experiences and thoughts. He allowed the collective brilliance of all the captains to come through. After he had heard his men and shared his own thoughts, the battle plan was drawn. Nelson's intent was clear.

The 'how'

How they were to conduct themselves and work with each other was clear. Why this particular battle was so important was understood by all. He had gained, once again, the total loyalty and commitment of his leaders by creating a specific clarity and aligned culture – not by telling, but through engagement.

At any stage in the heat of the battle, each of the captains had only one simple question to answer: 'Will my next action support the central mission?' Each captain could then have answered himself with, 'If they do, then I'm free to act.'

It did not matter that their leader was not there. They knew his intent. They knew they were truly empowered to act. They had clarity and a cohesive fleet-wide culture that would give them confidence in themselves and the other ships.

Nelson created a clarity that allowed people to feel totally empowered to act to support the vision, so when he wasn't there it actually didn't matter. Imagine that Nelson had been a control freak, the person with the BlackBerry whom all the decisions came to. Once he got shot we'd all have ended up speaking French or Spanish and it would be a very different world from the one we're in now. However, because he was totally aware of the need to create that picture, that clarity, allow everybody to be committed to what happened, this, crucially, meant he didn't have to be there to supervise. If the skippers had been compliant with – as opposed to committed to – Nelson's plan, we'd have lost the collective brilliance of all the experience of all the captains, and, when Nelson had gone, the plan would have fallen apart.

And on my yacht, if we had not taken the time and effort in creating our culture and putting speed first, we could not have attacked the first storm and hence the second, third and Hurricane Michael. Never make light of vision and values.

These are what take you through the tough times and steer you in the good times to ensure that you're ready to do whatever needs to be done.

What I learned from the Nelson story I applied to my own crew and have continued to apply to all the teams I build and with all the organisations I advise, and that is two things. First, you cannot create a high-performing team or organisation without a clearly defined and agreed clarity of direction and vision and a culture everyone can emotionally engage with. Second, you need to understand your role as the leader in the creation of this culture. It is not to direct and enforce, but to guide, facilitate and enable.

A culture cannot stand on its own. It needs:

- to sit with the clarity of vision
- to sit with a plan of action
- to reinforce the identity

They say culture eats strategy for breakfast. But culture needs strategy to breathe. The big take-away from this chapter is that proactively setting the right culture and clarity is your get-out-of-jail-free card.

If, in advance of a pressured situation, you have set the culture that a threat is no more or less than an opportunity in disguise, and if you have a defined clarity, culture and identity for the team, this allows you to approach storms (actual and metaphorical) with the correct mindset and will enable success.

And, if you really need any more convincing about the need for a coherent culture aligned to a vision, then look at the hysterical Monty Python clip about the Silly Olympics and the '100-metre dash for people with no sense of direction' – it's on YouTube – that ain't the way to win medals!

Key Learnings

- Forget to define your team's clarity and culture at your peril!

- A high-performance culture requires clarity, character and identity.

- Character drives behaviour.

- Character changes when the individual is under stress.

- Clarity sets direction.

- Shared identity encourages team buy-in and alignment.

- Facilitate the team to own the culture.

- You cannot enforce a culture.

EXERCISE: HOW TO CREATE A COHERENT CULTURE

There is no practical exercise related to this chapter as creating a culture takes a serious amount of time, effort and commitment. It must be done, but it must not be done lightly.

Having a coherent culture is vital. The research to support the performance impact of creating a values-based organisation is massive. Understanding, agreeing to and aligning around the 'why', the purpose, is so absolutely core but so frequently forgotten as we tend to focus on numbers and deliverables without meaning.

Creating the clarity of vision, direction and action with an aligned culture delivers the most powerful performance. Your identity is the window the world looks through to judge who you are.

The *leader* should not 'create the culture': the *people* should, with the leader's input and guidance. Everyone in your organisation needs to get involved in creating the culture. This is ⟶

not a top-down exercise: it is real life, with real people trying to fulfil self-worth – as are you.

The work needed to create a clarity, culture and identity is much. It is a long journey but worth the effort.

When I work on effecting large-scale cultural change I typically engage with an organisation for 12–18 months facilitating the cultural transformation; this is what I do:

DISCOVERY: With a mix of online surveys and selected interviews, a discovery of current and future state is undertaken that will inform the cultural development. It is important to understand and agree the starting point, establish the desire to move away, establish the 'to be' position and understand the drivers to move towards. Frequently I use the High Performance Organisation work by Professor André de Waal that I alluded to earlier in this book. It is excellent work that creates an easily understood and bought-into reason for the transformation – everyone can aspire to high performance no matter what motivational base they may have.

EXECUTIVE BOARD: Even though this is not a top-down trans-formation, the top needs to be at 'best function' and truly aligned. The strategic intent needs to be developed and owned by every member of the leadership team. The leadership team need to be visually and actively champions of the culture and clarity. An intense, three-day, off-site clarity-creation event followed by a series of monthly one-day meetings and one-to-one coaching has the biggest and quickest impact. Part of the outcome of these interactions is clarity and acceptance of the 'purpose' of the executive board in focusing on collective strategic decisions.

MANAGEMENT: This team need more help than any other area. They are driven and measured hard on delivery, so, even with the best will in the world, frequently become the 'clay layer', imper-vious to change. What does work is an intense series of 'kick-off' events with smaller cross-functional groups, followed by an 18-month programme of quarterly dialogue (QD) with the ⟶

whole team. The QD comprises four elements: a 'Show and Tell' an 'Investment', a 'Next Steps' and a 'Relationship Development' social event to close. The most powerful way to express this cadence of events is by using the expression 'wisdom.' These are Wisdom Dialogues, with 3 steps – Sharing Wisdom, Growing Wisdom and Wisdom Actions.

The Sharing Wisdom 'Show and Tell' is powerful in that it prompts action beforehand; it shares best practice; and it gives courage to try. The Growing Wisdom 'Investment' is a way of paying back and acknowledging the impact that these people make and will include elements of leadership development aligned to the cultural transformation. The Wisdom Action 'Next Steps' element creates a commitment and cohesion to a series of actions aligned to the clarity and culture that will impact on the whole organisation. The 'Relationship Development' element is both a thank-you and a vital part of breaking down functional barriers and creating relationship across the whole at all levels.

CHAMPIONS: I frequently create a group of 'cultural champions' that span the organisation covering all geographies and levels who will 'own' the cultural change and become the eyes, ears and conduit for meaningful dialogue with the leadership team. This team may well consist of 'top talent' and become a method to engage with and invest in the leaders of the future.

CASCADE: The cascade is not done as a *fait accompli*. The principle is that it must be leader-led and is to gain engagement, commitment and feedback on impact. The design and delivery here are critical. Creating a culture is not only top-down, but bottom-up as well.

MOMENTUM: This is a long and twisting road. There will also be a suspicion from the teams that this will not last. Many are 'initiative-weary', as leaders tend to be great at starting something but not completing. Any leadership group will have only *one chance* to effect a cultural change. If you do not ⟶

get it right first time, then there will be no second time in your tenure.

COMMUNICATION: You will need to create a communications programme to support the new culture. This is more than posters, but posters are an important part. The creation of a message that can be used with all stakeholders is an important part.

HUMAN RESOURCES: There is a saying that 'what you measure is what you deliver'. This is true for cultural change, too. Your organisation will need to review all of its 'human processes' to ensure they support the new culture: reward and recognition mechanisms, recruitment, induction, hierarchy.

A key input into creating a coherent culture is the output from the 'Big Journey'. This is a very powerful way to create that awareness of values mapping and resultant commitment needed to make it stick.

Notes

_____

_____

_____

_____

_____

_____

_____

_____

_____

_____

_____

_____

CHAPTER 10

DISCIPLINE AND CHALLENGE

At the centre of a Compassionate Leader lies self-discipline. Discipline creates freedom and allows choice. Success and achievement are all about internal discipline. To me, there's little point investing time in learning and development if discipline is absent. Without the discipline to follow an idea through to its completion, it is a wasted effort.

It doesn't sound sexy, I know, but winning is all about discipline; success at all levels starts with internal discipline.

Discipline is fun!

I like to win. There is so much more enjoyment in success. Of course, we learn through mistakes, but we grow through success. Success breeds success. Success breeds confidence, but success demands discipline.

You could argue that a number of different factors contribute to success and you would be right: planning, proper resourcing, competence, commitment, a vision, good communications, the right idea. You need them all, but, if you do not have the 'discipline' to follow process, stay strategic, commit to the plan, be a role model, be consistent, then the rest will be irrelevant.

In essence, it is 'discipline' that unlocks all the other factors and enables success. There is no doubt that discipline is key in everything we do. Not only is this true in the context of leadership and achievement as a team, but also in the concepts of personal achievement and in the ideas of completion.

Can you imagine Usain Bolt having a cracking start in the Olympic 100-metres final, and then wandering off the track at 80 metres, lacking the discipline to complete? His euphoria, just like ours, comes from completion – breaking the tape. Discipline is about getting things done, and it allows us to enjoy the whole emotion of completion and success. I see so many senior leadership teams who are great at starting stuff – in fact they are superb at starting stuff – but do they have the discipline to stick with it to the end, embed it and see if it works? Do they heck! They are off on the next big thing while the poor old staff just look up in despair. Sounds familiar, doesn't it? If you are one of those leaders, reflect awhile and consider the impact of your lack of discipline.

Let me make this memorable for you and share with you a story about discipline, and why it's important in the context of success and Compassionate Leadership.

The North Pole

I'll take you back to my expedition to the Magnetic North Pole, the Polar Race, the first race to either pole where the competitors were to start at the same time in the same place. When Robert Falcon Scott and Roald Amundsen raced to the South Pole, it was not a race: Scott was set up for manpower and discovery and Amundsen created a team just for speed. With *this* race, though, a line would be drawn in the snow and a starting gun would puncture the air. You would know where you stood all the time, whether you were in the lead or had lost it. There would be no hiding place.

Before the race, we spent time, of course, working on our clarity, culture and identity. Our identity was to come from our main sponsor – the Initial Style Conference Centres. As a team we agreed how we were to be and what we wanted to achieve.

Our private and public statement of intent, our clarity, was, 'To complete and enjoy a safe and effective race – achieving first place through a total team approach.'

We had made a public statement that 'We intend to win.' And not just win, but to lay a marker for the years to come. *Saying* you want to win is the easiest thing in the world. 'I want to win.' Easy. Go on, say it! But to live 'winning', to actually make it happen, that is tough!

'Achieving first place'. A bold statement indeed, especially as, three months before the race, I had never donned a pair of cross-country skis. I had a lot to learn.

I have been downhill skiing for many years, on piste, off piste (sometimes deliberately) – and plenty of after-piste of course. However, cross-country skiing was something altogether new. I teamed up with two ex-Royal Marines – Britain's elite fighting force whose values of courage, unity, determination, adaptability, unselfishness, humility, cheerfulness, professional standards, fortitude and commando humour, when linked with an iron will to win, great fitness and discipline, make a formidable capability. What a great culture!

The value I like the most, and I see it deeply embedded in the Marine psyche, is that of 'humour in the face of adversity'. No matter where you are or what predicament you are in, a Marine will crack a joke – nothing about good taste of course!

The team were led by Chris McLoed. He's a highly decorated Royal Marines officer, having been awarded the coveted Sword of Honour, Commando medal and a whole chest full more of campaign medals. He's eight years my junior, as fit as a butcher's dog and an excellent skier. The second Royal Marine and incredibly impressive character was Phil Ashby. He was awarded the Queen's Gallantry Medal, having displayed amazing heroics in Sierra Leone. His book, *Unscathed*, telling the story of his escape from the rebels of Sierra Leone, is a bestseller and when the film comes out, as I am sure it will, it will be a box-office hit. Phil was in the Mountain Leader Training

Cadre of the Royal Marines. They used to teach the Marines how to ski, survive and move in polar conditions. A brilliant skier, eight years my junior and, like Chris, as fit as a butcher's dog. (By the way, a butcher's dog is always given the best cuts of meat, hence the fitness!)

So I can sense that the first question forming in your mind at this point is, 'Hang on! Why is Manley in the team in the first place? He can't ski, he's a sailor, he's older, he's not as fit.' A very good question, and one that I talk more about in another part of the book. For now, I was there because I was not one of them. I was not an ex-Royal Marine, I was not SBS-trained, etc. I was different and that is a good thing. I am not a bad navigator, I can generally find my way around – and back again. I am annoyingly chirpy and optimistic. Even with a hangover I'm happy. Fun for me, but can be very annoying for my wife. A bit of enthusiasm and optimism is going to be a good thing high in the Arctic: 'Come on, chaps, another day in frozen hell. Hurrah!'

Given that we had publicly stated our intention not just to win but to lay down a marker for future races, clearly we were going to have to be special to achieve this.

We trained, we prepared, we planned, we got it wrong, we got it right, it was all starting to come together. Chris and Phil managed a weekend in Scotland, then as a team we trained in the French Alps and lastly in Norway. At times the weather was too benign, so we slept in the day and trained at night to try to get a true sense of the challenge we were about to undertake.

How was it? Did we win?

The whole story of that race is a book in itself. It was magical. I loved it. It was all I had hoped it would be. We encountered polar bears – a couple of skirmishes as we argued the difference in perception of where we both stood relatively on the food chain, but they were resolved without bloodshed. It was cold, it was tough and it was relentless.

But we did win – and we did it in style at a blistering pace, averaging over 35 miles a day with an elapsed time of 10 days and 9 hours. Often, when I tell this story, I put our success down to two factors: luck and ignorance.

We were lucky with the weather – only one really bad day – and we were lucky with the polar bears. And ignorance? I was ignorant of the level of pain I should be in and the Royal Marines did not seem to feel pain, so I thought this was normal.

But the real differences, the bits that enabled us to use our strength and determination to effect, were our discipline and our challenge. The key element to our success was internal discipline, with a secondary philosophy of 'challenge everything'. To deliver extraordinary results, no matter in what field, requires these two overarching elements.

Let me explain. Internal discipline means being totally aware of all your actions, your mental state and thinking and the impact on those around you. It means being disciplined to ensure that all thought and actions remain focused on delivering high performance. This primary thinking creates the secondary thinking of 'challenge everything'. Is the traditional way of getting something done actually the best way of completing it? If it isn't, then change it. Just because it *has* been done that way, it doesn't mean it must *always* be done that way. Be disciplined enough to challenge success as well as failure (see my earlier accounts of attacking Hurricane Michael and the next storm that crossed our path only three days later, Tropical Storm Nadine).

For us on our race to the Magnetic North Pole the external manifestation of our internal and team discipline became a constant reminder to ourselves and a statement to the rest of the world, and allowed us to challenge even the sun and the stars – time itself! We didn't actually run a 24-hour day. I did not want 24 hours. We created a 20-hour day. Fortunately for us, the sun never set. It was bouncing along the horizon all day and all night long, so we were free to choose the number of hours in the day to suit us. We chose 20 hours because it made for a more effective physiological and psychological tempo.

Twenty-hour days meant we didn't rest too long. Too long a

rest and our blood sugar levels would drop too much through fasting, our muscles would cramp, seize and potentially atrophy (our bodies would eat into our own muscles in their attempt to rebalance energy stores). Nor would we march for too long with our 20-hour day. The longer we marched, the greater the imbalance between energy in and energy out. There is a limit to how much you can actually eat or your body can process. Even with consuming 8,500 calories per day we were losing weight fast. If we marched too long it would mean our bodies would have to eat their own muscles and use up muscular carbohydrates and fats so quickly that we couldn't replace them. A 24-hour day would not work. We had to 'challenge'. So we did!

Given all of this psychological and physiological knowledge, 20 hours made sense. We split up our 20-hour day into the following structure:

- 13 hours of marching
- 2 hours of cooking, melting ice for water, personal administration (and there's enormous discipline needed around that as well!)
- 4 hours for sleep – no more, no less
- 1 hour for breakfast, melt more ice, sort our kit out before . . . (back to the top)

In our 13 hours of marching we did 90 minutes nonstop, followed by a break, then a further 90 minutes, followed by a break, and so the day went on relentlessly following this routine to completion. At each break the lead changed. If you were at the front you had the critical job of choosing the best path through the bergs and broken ice; you set the pace and you always, always looked over your shoulder to check on your mate behind (the first rule of convoy driving is that it is the responsibility of the car in front always to have view of the car behind, and so it is with polar expeditions). If you were Number Two, your job was a sense check, keeping tabs on the navigation, making sure that Number One was true to course as he tried to find the best route. Number Two also looked over his shoulder to check on Number Three. If you were at the back, you were 'resting', having just spent 90 minutes as Number One. You could switch off for a while, preserve some energy and focus on your body. But Number Three also looked over his shoulder to check for . . . polar bears. So I reckon Number Three was, in fact, the toughest place to be.

Psychologically, we could easily break down any element of the day into threes, allowing us to create smaller targets to maintain the psychological boost of achievement and closure.

But I need to tell you more about these breaks, for it was the breaks that became our external manifestation of internal discipline. If I said to you, 'Let's have a five- or ten-minute break,' how long would that actually be? There's no discipline around it and it becomes a nebulous concept. Generally, what happens is that people take breaks for as long as they want, or until they get bored around the coffee machine, or until the person who gave them the break in the first place gets upset that they haven't rushed back in to hear more pearls of wisdom.

For us, during our race to the North Pole, we had seven-minute breaks. Seven is exact, it's angular, it's a prime number. If I now say to you that we will have a seven-minute break, how long do you think a seven-minute break is? Exactly seven minutes! That, for us, was the biggest statement. We never, ever, ever broke the seven-minute rule. It was there to remind us about internal discipline with an external, visible manifestation.

Everything we did, we did with the seven-minute-break philosophy in mind. This philosophy is about so much more than taking a break: it means that, when you get in from 13 hours of skiing and you're absolutely exhausted, you don't just collapse in a heap in the tent and go to sleep with your soggy boots and shoes on – a guaranteed way to get injured. You actually strip off inside the tent, clean your feet, powder your toes, check all your nooks and crannies – 'personal administration', as we termed it!

It has to be said, but when challenging yourself in such a way it is often the case that the things we take for granted normally are the most important physically and psychologically. One of the nicest feelings after drying your feet was sliding on your 'tent boots'— basically, little sleeping bags just for your feet. Exquisite!

But all this 'personal admin' takes time. You are mentally and physically exhausted. You have nothing left in you but you must do it, because if you don't do it you get into trouble. This is 'internal discipline'.

To me, success and achievement are all about internal discipline, whether it is during an expedition to the North Pole or during a weekly progress meeting. Without this, all else becomes meaningless and ineffective.

You may think this all sounds great but are asking, 'How am I going to apply the seven-minute-break principle? It takes more than seven minutes to get a coffee.'

Well, let's take the seven-minute-break concept as an example. There are countless organisations in which I have incorporated the concept of the seven-minute break. First, it's important to explain why you want to introduce the seven-minute break into your organisation, detailing the whole story of internal discipline and success. You can tell my story if you wish, or have one of your own.

Second, agree what it means. For example it may not literally mean seven minutes for coffee, since you might have to have fourteen minutes for coffee, made up of two consecutive seven-minute breaks. Or 23 minutes. It is the *principle* of 'discipline', not the rigid adherence to the clock.

Third, monitor the discipline around the seven-minute break. You watch, or someone watches and agrees a time to come back in. Preferably, if you have sold the concept well enough and your people have bought into it, there will be no need to call them back: they will naturally come.

Fourth, challenge the status quo. Why have a meeting beginning and ending on the hour, and then another starting on the hour? You're doomed to failure. Why not have a 47-minute meeting starting at 12 minutes past the hour? Putting a bit of angularity or awkwardness into your diary and into your day promotes focus – and discipline.

Seven-minute breaks are all about internal discipline, setting yourself up to succeed. There are so many ways that you can apply it in business. Stop for a second now and think, What will my seven-minute break be? What external statement and internal reminder can I create to instil the concept of internal discipline and high performance?

EXERCISE: CHALLENGE 20/24

Here is a challenge for you. You will need to do a 'cultural audit' and a 'governance audit' at least. Have a look at all the meetings, processes, systems and the culture of your organisation and apply the 20/24 principle. Can we do it differently and better? Does 'it' align to our strategic intent (our clarity)? What is blocking us and what enables us? Challenge everything – especially yourself and your own behaviour!

EXERCISE: SEVEN-MINUTE BREAK

Stop for a second now and think, What will my seven-minute break be? What external statement and internal reminder can I create to instil the concept of internal discipline and high ➝

performance? Look at the times you do take breaks. Are they disciplined? Do your meetings start on the hour and last an hour? Make them different, awkward: start at ten past, finish at ten to.

Discipline starts at home

We all need to be strong with our own internal discipline. This is true in any walk of life, whether it's from a leadership perspective, working with a business team or a sporting team; whether it's in relationships at home and with friends and family; or whether it is for our own hobbies and communities. If we can be strong with our own internal discipline first, how we lead ourselves and how we exhibit that behaviour externally, then that has an impact on everybody around us. Your own internal discipline allows you to achieve; it allows you to compete and complete; it allows you to fulfil a sense of purpose for whatever you want to do.

Internal discipline can also be used effectively in groups of people in how it influences how other people behave. Any behaviour you exhibit gives other people permission to behave likewise, particularly if you're in a senior position where the concept of 'senior amplification' is very real.

If you are living a seven-minute philosophy, if you are extolling the virtues of internal discipline and you're providing evidence of such in the way you behave with other people, it becomes infectious. They then can take on that same evidence and those same behaviours themselves, and internal discipline tends to become a way of life and part of the culture you're creating. So discipline enables you to fulfil whatever it is you want to achieve, whether it's influencing yourself or influencing other people, in business or in life in general.

When you look at all the lessons and learning in this book and how to apply it, you can do one of two things:

- you can read the book and carry on as you were; or
- you can have the internal discipline to actually start making changes in your behaviour and your thinking

For you to develop a stronger sense of 'internal discipline' or if you are trying to influence others to adopt the seven-minute philosophy, you have a sales job to do in order to tap into your and their intrinsic, internal motivation.

Don't be the master of the clock. Instead, let them own their own. You will need to sell the self-interest to yourself and to others and you will need to motivate them to join your thinking, and you can do that only with an accepted power base.

Clearly, the seven-minute philosophy and the 20/24 principle are two UMU ways of thinking and acting that you can adopt now, with no delay, in any walk of life you choose.

Throughout this book we discuss the importance of your role as a 'Compassionate Leader' in modelling the behaviour you want to see – slack boss, slack team! If you don't challenge, then neither will they.

CASE STUDY: THE IMMOBILE MOBILE

I was supporting a large retail organisation that was trying to change its whole way of behaving. Previously, the value set was that the management didn't really listen or didn't really empower or enable the staff to engage. As a result, they weren't getting collective brilliance and ideas ⟶

from the staff. When talking to the staff I heard expressions such as, 'I had my fingers burned, so I just keep my head down nowadays.' Part of the problem with the old culture was that the leadership were too busy on task-oriented activity – email, their own busy lives, what 'had' to be done right now on the floor – rather than on the people or rela- tionship activity.

One of the leaders, on the back of a course I ran to inculcate the new values, said that he would never again take his mobile phone onto the shop floor. Previously, the leader would go onto the shop floor to engage with the staff, meet his people, understand them, get to know what work was like. It sounds great. But then his phone would ring and he would answer it, making his phone the priority over his staff. So he never got to speak to the people and the staff never thought they could be listened to by him, and, by association, by the leadership in general. Nine months on, the discipline he had undergone to ensure that he never had his phone with him on the shop floor, and the impact that had, was enormous. It meant that people now approached him, both customers and staff. It's only a small behaviour change, and having the disci- pline to follow it through is the hard part. Yet consistency can be achieved and it will have a large impact.

CASE STUDY: WHEN 10 MINUTES EARLY IS LATE

When on the BT Global Challenge, and inculcating the values we wanted, we spoke about punctuality. Imagine how impor- tant it must be mid-ocean. You're 1,700 miles away from land; you've been at sea for two and a bit weeks deep ⟶

in the Southern Ocean; it's cold and you've been on watch, on shift for four hours between midnight and 4 a.m. As you approach 4 a.m., you're cold, wet, hungry, tired and possibly frightened, and the person who's meant to relieve you is late. Imagine the impact that will have on you, on your own personal space and on your relationship with the other person. What does it say about being late? It says, 'I don't respect you; I don't value you; I'm more important than you.' It says that collectively we're not anything, just individuals.

So, clearly, punctuality is very, very important. What I didn't want to do as the leader of the group was make the rules. If I made the rules and we looked at what our culture is, then I had to be the policeman of the rules. If the team set the rules, they could self-police. One of the rules, or behaviours if you like, that the team came up with was to be 'on time, all the time'.

I challenged my team with, 'Well, that sounds great, but what does it actually mean? What is the behaviour behind, "on time, all the time"?'

After much discussion, debate, and even after much practice, they agreed that 10 minutes early was late. That may sound contradictory, but you should be on deck 15 minutes before handover. If you're tired, if you've had only a few hours' sleep, there's the temptation to stay snuggled up in your sleeping bag. But the reality was that people had to get up 45 minutes before they had to be on watch, to have enough time to get ready and make sure they were always up on deck 15 minutes or more before they had to be, to ensure it was a good handover and show their respect to the team. A classic example of discipline and of inculcating a culture of success.

Smelly Loos!

There's another example of discipline that has an enormous impact on others, and, when visiting businesses and companies I use it as an indicator of the general 'health' of an organisation. And that's the toilets. This example could quite happily fit in Chapter 9 on culture, but I include it here because at the core of this example lies personal discipline as well as respect for others.

As I tour companies early in our relationship I always find time to 'visit the heads', as we say at sea. To check out the loos. Some are a disgrace, worse than railway toilets. What does it tell me? That people are lazy, ill-disciplined and disrespectful. They clearly do not care about their colleagues, what impact leaving an untidy loo will have on the person following, what perception might be left with the client, customer or visitor. The first element is that lack of respect, but the second is their own personal discipline (as well as hygiene)! Maybe I am slightly anal (ha!) about it, but I would hate the person using the toilets after me to think that I am a disgrace – wouldn't you? With these types of organisations, I tend to dwell longer and dig deeper to find out what the culture is really like, where else they may not be applying the seven-minute break philosophy.

And tidy toilets? Well, they may just be rich enough to afford a cleaner, so it is not always a fair indication.

Key Learnings

- Discipline is key to success and achievement. There's no point starting something if you're not going to finish it.

- Discipline starts with the individual. Internal discipline will breed discipline in those around you.

- Seven-minute breaks are a manifestation of discipline. Try it!

- There is self-interest in everything we do. Accept it. Understand it. Use it.

- To influence others to achieve a joint outcome, look to their self-interest. Accept it. Understand it. Use it.

- The choice is yours: have discipline, or don't have discipline. What is your self-interest in the outcome?

Notes

_____

_____

_____

_____

_____

_____

_____

_____

_____

_____

_____

_____

_____

CHAPTER 11

_____

COMMUNICATION

It was mid-ocean on the first leg of the amazing race around the world – the BT Global Challenge. We had covered some good miles in the preceding days and were now settling in sweetly to the rhythm of life at sea, having left port some 10 days before. We had spent much time before leaving understanding how we were going to work together, our purpose, vision and values, our clarity and culture and, specifically and vitally, how we were to communicate with each other.

Poor communication can add so much to poor performance and create incredible tension. It is hard enough in a normal and relatively quiet environment to be really understood, but at sea, with the noise, confusion and distraction, it can be nigh on impossible. We thought we had it sorted and, as the leader, I was quite content and not expecting any basic communication issues. We all had our places on the yacht and the manner in which all the crew were developing made me feel good. Sometimes as a leader it is good just to sit back and observe, and, when it is all running as it should, it creates a warm feeling that all is well with the world. In fact, it is vital that leaders do 'sit back and observe' – not to do so is not being a leader.

As I was watching my team work together with a smug feeling of self-congratulation on a job well done, I noticed a classic case of assumption. Let me explain what I mean and how much damage it can cause. A yacht is a complex system of interrelated areas – 'parts of ship', each specific but each needing the others. I do not believe there is any finer example of ultimate teamwork than when a crew tame the wind and waves to power a large yacht.

For the 'land lubbers' amongst you perhaps a short introduction to the two specific areas and associated roles that form the basis for this event would help. The area just behind the mast is known as 'the snake pit'. That's for a good reason, as there are 21 bits of string that all end up there – all the ropes that hoist the sails, fly the spinnaker and do all actions save the actual trimming of the sail itself, and the 'runners' (ropes out the back that help hold the mast up). To work in the snake pit takes a certain type of person, with good spatial awareness and a logical mind. It has to be a tidy person, too.

In the cockpit there are the 'trimmers', who, as the name suggests, trim the sails for optimum performance in relation to wind strength and angle. The trimmers have to be able to focus for long periods, always attending to the signs of sail performance and never, for one second, being distracted from trying to make the yacht go faster. Communication between the snake pit and the trimmers is clearly key for speed.

Tesco was trimming the head sail (the one at the front) and needed the Professor in the snake pit to increase the tension in the front of the sail – to 'grind on the halyard', as it is known.

In your mind, picture the scene. The wind is building, the sea growing. All around you there is activity and conversations as others play their part. Spray is now coming on board and reaching as far as the helmsman at the back of the boat. The snake pit is by now a wet and exposed place to be.

The conversation goes like this.

TESCO (shouting against the wind): Hey, Prof, could you wind on the yankee halyard a touch, please?

The PROFESSOR says nothing. His head is down. He's busy in the snake pit.

TESCO: Hey, Prof, could you wind on the yankee halyard?

The PROFESSOR still says nothing, but is clearly busy.

TESCO (his tone changing and clearly getting frustrated, voice raised): Hey, Prof, wind on the yankee!

PROFESSOR (annoyed, shouting): All right, all right, I heard you first time. Can't you see I'm busy? Stop shouting at me.

Problem? Assumptions all round. Tesco assuming he was heard and then ignored. Professor assuming that Tesco could see he was busy and would get to his request as soon as he could.

The outcome? Two people now annoyed with each other and the rest of the crew feeling tense, too, the boat not now being sailed at maximum potential.

Then I joined in. 'Whoa, hold on, chaps. What happened there? What should have happened? Let's start that dialogue again.'

You always have options as the leader. I could have just observed and ignored it, thinking, They'll sort it out. I could have interjected and possibly sided with the Professor: 'Steady on, Tesco, can't you see the Prof's busy?' Or sided with Tesco: 'Come on, Prof, hurry up.' Or I could use this as a superb coaching opportunity for the whole crew. That way, we would all learn, the problem would not arise again, emotions would be more level and the crew, hence the boat, would perform better both in that moment and in the long term.

To understand when a true 'coaching moment' arises is part of the skills of a highly conscious Compassionate Leader, and to commit the time to it is all part of the picture. It would have been quicker in the moment to have done nothing, but how much time did I save in the long run by my coaching intervention? What 'return' did I receive on my 'investment'? Stacks!

So we stopped and discussed as a crew what should have happened. The Professor, if he had heard the request, should have acknowledged. Tesco, with no acknowledgement from the Professor, should not have assumed he had been heard. It really was a simple as that. With the attitude of 'no assumptions', the communication would have worked, the tension would never have arisen and the focus on performance would not have been lost. But the 'no assumptions' needs to be part of the wider culture of the boat, so all understand and have a common expectation of how a dialogue is to work.

There and then, we adjusted our understanding of what good communication looked like and developed our 'rules'. Our Team Large culture was evolving, as all good cultures must.

Aside from the lessons on communication there are more learnings in that one little vignette.

- Any 'cultural or behavioural rules' you may have created can always be developed and improved – nothing is ever set in stone.
- If I had not been observing, the lesson would have been lost, the problem would have remained, with morale and performance both suffering as a consequence. Leadership is about continual awareness and observation; heads-up leadership, Compassionate Leadership is about getting 'off the dance floor and on to the balcony'.
- By including all the crew, not just the two protagonists in the debate on resolution, the 'inclusive coaching' created a good understanding and acceptance of the modified 'rule'. I could have just stopped the conversation, stated how they should communicate and left it at that, but then it would have been my rule and I would have had to police it.

The lessons on communication from this simple conversation are the following.

- never assume your message has been heard or understood
- always acknowledge communication, even if you cannot act on it immediately
- effective communication is, in essence, dialogue

The anchor for this learning? Just remember the story and think, Am I acting like the Professor or like Tesco? Have I assumed? Have I acknowledged?

Let's break from stories of sailing and look more closely at communication in the round. I have some questions I would like you to ponder.

What is the purpose of communication?

What's the point? Why do we communicate (and, boy, don't we do a lot of it!)? Email, text, online chats, Facebook, Twitter, letters, notes, messages, shouting, carrier pigeons, talking, whispering, gesticulating, direct, indirect. We receive by sight, sound and touch. We look at the word, hear the tone and, consciously or unconsciously, we are influenced by the body language. But why? To what end?

In simple terms, *communication is to create change*. By communicating we are sharing our information, opinions, thoughts, thus trying to effect change in others – a change of opinion, a change of awareness, a change in action or thinking, a change of understanding, a change of direction, but always a change.

So what does that mean? You know that, if you are to change anything, you need to understand where you are now and where you want to go, *whatever* it is you want to change. You need to know the start position and the destination. In other words, you need to know what the point of the conversation is.

Let's apply this to the situation we just looked at with Tesco and the Professor. Tesco wanted to change the Professor's actions and priorities. He wanted him to stop whatever he was doing and do his, Tesco's, bidding. The Professor's initial 'communication' was to stop Tesco from pestering him.

Let's give ourselves some basic rules and guidelines on effective communications. Before you open your mouth, write your missive or give the signal, pause and consider:

- Why am I communicating?
- What do I want to happen?
- What is the outcome I desire of this communication?

Think about it! Do I want them to change their actions, thinking, beliefs, perception? Do I want them to start something, continue something or stop something?

Be very, very conscious of that desired outcome. Be very clear in your mind what you want to achieve.

Use this thinking in all walks of life. When you next find yourself in a heated discussion with your teenage child, stop and contemplate what the outcome is that you desire. I have stopped many potential arguments simply by reflecting, mid-conversation, on what I wanted the outcome of the argument to be and realising that, actually, there would be no clear outcome, so . . . I just stopped.

Got it? Great! So now you know why you are communicating.

But wait. Hold on! Don't just broadcast. Stop again.

How will it land?

Before you march on with your delivery consider how will it be heard. What words will the receiver hear? What are their needs and motivations?

Do you remember how we dealt in Chapter 5 with the idea of filters? How some of us will 'hear' some words and others not? For me to 'hear' your communication, it needs to light my own fire. I must recognise 'me' within what you say. If not specifically, initially, to resonate with self-benefit, you must get past my natural filters for there to be a chance of any change. I'm a big-picture, broad-brush kind of chap. If you start off with the detail, I might fall asleep. Likewise, I have to think about who it is listening to you. You can't just spout off about your 'big dream' or general themes if my inner motivational filters require that you let me know more detail.

So think about whom you are communicating with. What are their motivations? Are they motivated by achievement, affiliation or influence, using David McClelland's Three Needs Theory? Do you paint the big picture, or focus on what is needed? Do you sell the benefits for them or for others? What are their immediate priorities or their long-term needs and wants? There are so many questions you need to answer before you start to broadcast. It's tough, this communication lark. You cannot just let fly. As with leadership, there is no such thing as a 'natural, effortless' communicator: you need to be aware. What mindset are they in with reference to the Parent–Adult–Child mindsets as articulated in the Transactional Analysis model I talk about later?

Knowing me, knowing you. To lead, you need to relate; to communicate, you need to relate; to relate, you need to be aware. The core thinking of Compassionate Leadership allows for great communication.

Have you ever thought or said, 'I've told them a thousand times, but they still don't get it'? Have you heard others say the same? We tend to blame the receiver for not listening or not understanding or being stupid. We point our fingers at the other and blame them. If you have had to tell them the same thing a thousand times and they still don't get it, then you do really need to look at yourself first and question your language and methods. You could then even ask them why they don't understand. Maybe it is you, not them!

I hear leaders say, 'I have no time for stupid.' But what arrogance! Who decides who is stupid? Are they stupid because they are not doing what you want? Are they stupid because they have a different way of looking at the world? Is 'different' stupid in your eyes? Think about it.

Do not blame the receiver. Look at yourself. If I have not understood your communication, it is not my fault: it is yours. You, not I, are to blame for my ignorance or my misunderstanding. Remember, you are the one who is trying to change something within me. The comprehension responsibility sits firmly with the broadcaster.

If the outcome they desire from any communication is not achieved, a good communicator, a good leader, a compassionate leader, will look at the way they have communicated first and endeavour to ensure that their communication has the best chance of landing by raising their awareness of the receiver and of the style and content of the communication.

How will I know I am understood?

'So now I can go and communicate, yes?' I hear you say. 'I know what I want to achieve. I know how best to communicate it so that the receiver will "hear" and "accept" what I have to say. Surely, now, Manley, I can go ahead, can't I? Please? Time's tight, don't forget, and I have much to do.'

But wait again! Yup, there's one more element of good communication to sort out before we open our mouths, press 'send' or stand up on that soap box.

How will you know you have been heard and understood? What are you expecting in return?

Tesco was expecting at the very least an 'OK, got it, will do, just let me finish this' from the Professor, or to see the action happening (though I do believe an affirmation beyond just the action helps), or even a hand signal, a thumbs-up.

What we had failed to do in all our discussions about good communication on the boat was to bring it down to real actions. We had spoken about how important communication was going to be and how we should talk with each other from a position of empathy and understanding. We had spoken about how hard it would be at times to communicate with the wind and the waves drowning all attempts at being heard. We even practised 'Benedictine' manoeuvres, where not a word was allowed to be spoken as we moved the yacht and changed the sails. We had set up a strong culture of briefing and debriefing at every evolution. But we had failed to take it to the next stage and to ask, 'So what does that style of communication look like? How do I act it?' We had failed to agree what a good conversation actually 'looks' like.

So do just that. Make it clear what you want in return. Ask for acknowledgement. Be open with it. Don't just put a 'read receipt' on your email. Check that your message was 'heard' and understood. And how best to do that? Don't just ask, 'Did you hear me?' or 'Do you understand?' Depending on the prevailing culture, it may take a strong person to say no to either of those questions without feeling exposed or being perceived as 'stupid'. Ask an 'open' question that solicits a considered response that clearly articulates comprehension. Share that you wish for a response.

Now you can communicate! No, wait, one more thing . . .

Preparation for communication

What can you do before you communicate to ensure your communication is understood and has the desired impact? It is not actually that complex, as there are only a small number of questions you must ask yourself before you fire away. Remember them?

- Be clear what you want to achieve – what is the desired outcome of your communication?
- Think about your audience and develop your understanding of the receiver(s) and their 'motivational filters'.
- Check how you want to ensure 'hearing' and 'understanding' have happened.

Then, and only then, decide on the best method to communicate.

The difference here is the level of 'consciousness' about how you communicate. Always be a 'conscious communicator'. There really should not be too many surprises in conscious communication.

Attitude

But what about preparing yourself? What attitude does a good conscious communicator have? Well, the right one, obviously, and it won't surprise you to learn that it's the same attitude as required for a Compassionate Leader too – they are one and the same. You may well be the best orator with what you perceive as a compelling argument, but if you enter the communication with the wrong attitude – that of ignorance, arrogance, knowing and not learning, assuming – then you will fail to create the lasting impact you wish.

Let's look closer, then, at attitude.

Do not assume

Never assume you have been heard; do not assume that you have been understood; and, crucially, do not assume you are right. Sending an email does not mean it has been received and understood. Telling a person what to do, and how, does not mean they understand the desired action and, more importantly, the reason why. Sticking a poster on the wall saying how people should behave does not mean they understand or buy into that.

You need confirmation not just on message reception, but on message comprehension: do they understand and can they commit to the desired change, action and activity, and the reason why?

Do not prejudge

Our prejudice gets in the way of so much. We look at the outside of a person and make a judgement of the inside.

I have already told you an embarrassing story about that concerning the two goths in Chapter 5. And I did it with some kids in the park. They wore hoodies and low-slung jeans and moped along with drooped shoulders. I dismissed them, thinking, Oiks, yobs!

What ignorance and arrogance, for, when I held the gate open for them as they entered the park as my kids and I left, they stopped, held the gate for me and said, 'Thank you.' Polite, considerate and compassionate. And I? Ignorant and full of prejudice – every day is a school day!

Do not judge

'I've told you a thousand times! Are you stupid?' 'I can't abide fools.' These and comments like them are heard all too often, especially by leaders in the corporate world. We tend to point at the 'receiver' rather than at ourselves when we don't get the reaction we want. If they have not heard or understood, don't just keep on repeating yourself and getting louder and showing your frustration (rather like an Englishman abroad), or you may well get the 'Yes' or 'OK' just to shut you up.

Change what and how you are communicating. Consider them and their needs, not you and yours. Think how your communication is 'landing' – create a dialogue and . . .

Be prepared to learn

Yes, learn! You never know – you may be wrong and they right. There are no absolutes, particularly in truths! We may believe that our course of action or our way of thinking is the 'one' truth or the 'one' way, the 'best' way. Remember, there is no energy in knowing but much energy in learning. (Remember our debate on 'expert' as a power base? See 'The five bases of power' in Chapter 7.) You may have done the job you are now asking others to do, but that does not mean that the way you did it was the best ever, or that other factors have not changed. The attitude of a good conscious communicator and Compassionate Leader is that of always being prepared to learn, to change your own path or thinking, by adopting the right mindset. Compassionate communication is a dialogue.

Adopt an 'adult' mindset

The best way to explain this is through the Canadian psychiatrist Eric Berne's excellent work, *Transactional Analysis in Psychotherapy*. (As always, my precis of Berne's work is just that – short and following the UMU principle. There are many books and papers on the work that I recommend you read.) We have a choice, as a conscious communicator, of adopting an 'adult' mindset and not that of a 'child' or 'parent'. Read the following descriptions on what these mindsets mean and reflect. Where are you? That last communication: How were you? Parent? Did you respond as a child? Where were they? Did you force them into a child state as you adopted the parent state? True communication comes when adult meets adult.

- PARENT: This is our 'taught' concept of life, our ingrained voice of authority formed by external events and influences. We act this by finger-pointing, adopting angry or dominant body language and positions. We may use words such as 'never' or 'always' and be judgemental, critical or patronising.
- CHILD: This is our 'felt' concept of life, the emotional response that can lead to feelings of anger or despair and 'unreason'. We see this through sad expressions, tantrums, shrugging shoulders, eye-rolling or squirming. We may hear from ourselves or others, 'I wish', 'Oh no, not again', 'Things never go right' and the use of superlatives or attempts to impress.
- ADULT: This is our 'thought' concept of life, our ability to think and reason and keep the parent or child under control. In the adult mindset we show interest and attention, and use nonthreatening posturing and language; we will ask for clarity and demonstrate reason and express things as opinion.

I can't, of course, explain in these few words the whole of Eric Berne's excellent work, or the development of it by other learned people that forms the modern thinking on transactional analysis. As a Compassionate Leader and conscious communicator you will be eager to understand more, and much has been written. Enjoy the learning journey.

Skills for the conscious communicator

So just what *are* the skills of a good compassionate, conscious communicator? So much has been written about them. You can attend so many courses focusing on the skills you need to be that elusive, effective communicator. But I believe that the first skill you need is to be able to set your attitude and strive to be that conscious communicator, and then work on developing the other skills.

So let us quickly look at the skills of a communicator. Depending on what advice you seek out, some skills are given greater importance, but my research would suggest the following list:

- listening
- questioning
- developing empathy/rapport
- giving feedback
- coaching
- storytelling

You can add your own, too, but let's reflect on my list for starters.

Listening

There is much about listening levels and active listening, both of which are key skills. However, if you have set the attitude, as we discussed above, then listening – real listening with a true intent to understand – can happen. No matter what 'skill' you acquire, if you do not adopt the right attitude you will not apply the skill, so focus on attitude and skill to support.

Remember the story I told you in Chapter 7 about the African chief's attitude to leadership? The demands on him were complex and highly charged with emotion, as much of the external influence on his people and their culture is not at all positive. I asked him what his best advice would be. 'It is simple,' he said. 'First, I listen.'

Questioning

Open, closed, simple, complex, direct, indirect? It can become confusing. So, create a conscious understanding of what the intent and desired outcome of your communication is. Ensure that your attitude is set to 'learn', not 'know', and create the dialogue required. Some simple rules to follow are: keep questions short, do not use multiple question sentences and do not prejudice or pre-answer the question within your question.

Developing empathy

We hear people talk about 'being in the other's shoes' as a way of describing empathy. A desire to understand the needs, motivations, wants of the other and their mindset is vital for good communication, but I would like to challenge you to take it one step further and develop compassion for the other.

I believe the word *compassion* is not well understood and becomes confused with empathy. Do you remember the Dalai Lama's definition? '"Empathy" is the desire to understand others, "compassion" is to act with positive intent on that understanding – compassion is at the heart of ethical behaviour.'.

Giving feedback

What does this really mean? For me, I see giving feedback as no more than having a conversation, a dialogue, with the intent to change something about the other. Sounds a bit similar to the whole purpose of communication. Specifically, it is a conversation about an act or behaviour, or a perception of that act or behaviour. It includes everything we have spoken about already, but with the addition of being more acutely aware of the environment in which you hold the conversation and with an agreed outcome.

Any comment on an act or perception of an act could well solicit an emotion within the other. Be aware of that and, in, say, a workplace situation, select an environment that will allow that response without fear that it will be overheard or judged by others. Be very aware of your and the other's mindset in terms of transactional analysis – feedback is about learning, not telling.

Coaching

Many great tomes have been written on the subject of coaching so I will not rewrite them here! Throughout this book you will have seen coaching presented as a style that a Compassionate Leader uses rather than as a specific activity in its own right. Earlier in this chapter I told the story of Tesco and the Professor miscommunicating on the yacht and how I used a coaching style to not only resolve the issue but also make it a collective learning opportunity. I also shared the story about mending the shed with my children in the chapter on power and influence. Again, this is an example of using coaching as a behaviour. Having the understanding of when to coach is vital but it cannot be a default style, though it can be a preferred style. Always answering a question with the question 'So what do you think?' can be incredibly annoying.

I have shared a superb model to use when coaching at the end of this chapter called the GROW model (suitably UMU of course!). The GROW model is more than just a model for specific coaching moments, it is a great question-structuring tool. I use it all the time; I share it with companies globally and apply it to my own coaching sessions. I suggest that you apply it to yourself first, as practice for working with others.

So what is coaching?

Here are some thoughts on what coaching is and what coaching is not:

- Coaching is reactive, flexible and enabling, not prescriptive or instructional. Coaching is nonjudgemental. Coaching helps people to develop and grow.
- Coaching is about getting the very best out of someone and enabling them to make decisions that will improve their work and their life.
- Coaching is a two-way process. Personal development for the coach is a huge aspect of learning coaching and all coaches find that they themselves grow whilst coaching.
- Coaching is different to training. Coaching draws out rather than puts in. It develops rather than imposes. It reflects rather than directs. Coaching is different to psychology, counselling or therapy. Coaching doesn't claim to have the answers. A coach's job is not to go over old ground, be past-orientated or to force-feed information, but to work with people to help them find the answers themselves.
- Coaching is not consulting. A consultant is a specialist in his or her field whereas a coach is a specialist in coaching, and need not be a specialist in any other field.
- Coaching is not advising. It is essential that coaches coach and do not give advice. There's a huge difference between coaching and advising. Coaching is centred around the person; whereas advising tends to be based on the beliefs, values and opinions of the adviser.

- Coaching is not mentoring, though part of mentoring may be coaching.
- Coaching is fun, great fun – I love it!

Storytelling

You know my thinking on this one. Stop telling people what for or what you know or the 'right' way to do things. Tell a story instead. Interest them, inspire them, let them have questions, let them place themselves within the story and let them tell the story themselves.

Traditionally, wisdom was always shared by the telling of stories or singing of songs. Parables, fables and everyday expressions such as 'cry wolf' show this. More enlightened, and most indigenous peoples still do, but in our 'developed' world we seem to think we know best, so have come to tell and direct. It never works so well; it is an intellectual message, a left-brain concept. And guess what? In this last paragraph, I have fallen into the 'telling trap' too! Perhaps I should have shared a story here!

How we receive information

There is much debate about how we interpret communications.

The psychology professor Albert Mehrabian has pioneered the understanding of communications since the 1960s. His theory is often used and is a superb guide. But care must be taken to understand the context of his research and findings. It was specifically about communications with a high level of 'emotional' content.

Mehrabian said that that 55 per cent of our communication comes from the body, including facial expressions; that sound accounts for 38 per cent, including the tone of our voice; and just 7 per cent comes from the words themselves.

You could simplify this by equating words to 'email', 'sound' to 'telephone' and 'body language' to a 'face-to-face'! In other words, being with the person, face to face, so you can receive all the information is the best way to gain the full emotional context of any communication. Over the phone you will be missing out on over half the information and with email potentially missing out on 93 per cent! To apply this thinking in a manner commensurate with being a Compassionate Leader would mean applying the John Adair leadership model to meetings; working on the more emotional relationship element when together and saving the less emotional information and business parts for remote communications.

The value of Mehrabian's theory relates to communications where there is a strong emotional content, when we are talking about emotions and feelings, and not just conveying unemotional information.

If the listener is trying to understand the motivation and emotion behind the words, then great emphasis is placed on observing how the speaker looks and sounds. In a management or leadership role, where the motivation and emotion have a great impact on outcomes and buy-in, this is important, and possibly more so in building relationships!

My good friend the superb communications expert Robin Kermode uses the sentence, 'I didn't steal that money' to demonstrate how we can change meaning through changing the focal point of a sentence (not sure what this particular sentence says about Robin)!

Let's look at different ways of saying that.

- *I* didn't steal that money (but someone did)
- I didn't *steal* that money (I only borrowed it)
- I didn't steal *that* money (I stole some other money)
- I didn't steal that *money* (but I did nick the bread)

I believe the best way to apply Mehrabian's superb theory is to say that, if I invest the time in face-to-face, I can build a better relationship and understanding, so any future emotional context in a phone call or an email is not lost. In other words, since they know my motivations, they won't confuse my message.

So, next time you can organise a face-to-face with someone or your team, don't just leap into the agenda and focus on the task. Remember John Adair's model on balanced leadership? When you are together, that is the time to develop the relationship, the understanding, the 'knowing you'. Do not waste the opportunity to garner 100 per cent of the information hidden in communication.

Dialogue

I want to complete this chapter on communication by sharing my distaste for the word *communication* and my favouring of the word *dialogue* in its place!

Whenever people speak about 'communication' I like to challenge them. 'We need to communicate more.' 'We need better communications.' 'We need more effective communications.' What does that mean? There are more than enough 'communications' out there. Do we really need any more?

How about we change that expression and say, 'We need more dialogue'; 'We need better dialogue'; 'We need more effective dialogue'? It changes the meaning completely. It transforms the attitude from expert teller to energetic learner; from blind blah-blah-blah to conscious communicator; from forcing compliance to gaining commitment; from any old leader to a Compassionate Leader.

Try it. See how it feels. See what change it makes right at the start. See how it helps you achieve the desired outcome and create that 'commitment' we all want.

EXERCISE: COMMUNICATION

Think when you have struggled to get your message across, or someone has misunderstood.

Create a communication checklist!

Communication	Acknowledgement	Assumption	Message landed?	Action
Town hall.	Good numbers present.	Had not checked if invitation received.	Think yes, good questions.	Disseminate action points, call team leader to discuss.

EXERCISE: BLIND COACHING

We've discussed coaching as one of the key skills of a Compassionate Leader – the ability to unlock what is within your team, build trust, gain commitment and tap into the 'collective brilliance' that is latent within every team and every person. It is an 'unlocking' behaviour and the way to accelerated learning. It is so important to be able to do it and do it well.

I didn't say it was a panacea. There is a time and a place, and the time for you to give it a go is here and now.

There is no need for you to be the 'expert'. By definition, if we are coaching ourselves it is because we are not sure of the direction or facts, and, if we are coaching others, and if they can come up with the answer, then *they* own it, not you, and they then commit to it.

You should prepare for this blind coaching session by contemplating a goal that you want to achieve. Anything! It could be about work, or about life. What do you really want to achieve? Stop and reflect. Write it down here now.   ➡

My Blind Coaching Goal

_____

_____

_____

_____

_____

_____

_____

_____

_____

_____

_____

We will use the GROW model, GROW standing for goal, reality, options and way ahead (or will). The G and R bits may well be iterative, for as you discover where you really are now, you may need to modify the goal – or certainly ratify it.

Goal

What specifically do you want to achieve?

What will success look like?

How much personal control or influence do you have over achieving your goal?

When do you want to achieve it by?

How will you know when you have achieved it?

How will you feel when it's been achieved?

What will it do for you?

How important is it for you?

Can you do it? With or without others? ⟶

OK, so now you should have clarity about exactly what it is you are striving for, the reason why you are going for it and the benefits and change it will bring to you. And you should have a feeling that you can get there, but you may need some help.

So let's look at where we are now ...

Reality
What is happening now?
Why do you want to move from here?
What is involved (directly and indirectly)?
How is this affecting you?
What are you observing about this?
What are you assuming about this?
How do you feel about this?
What have you done about this so far?
What results did that produce?
What is holding you back from finding a way forward?

You should be thinking, Not only do I now know where I want to go, but I also strongly believe that I don't want the status quo to remain; I don't want to stay where I am. You would have 'felt' or realised a 'discomfort' about your present state and an 'excitement' about the potential of where you are heading.
So, how are we going to get there? Let's look at our ...

Options
So what options are there? Go crazy, think about all the ways this can be done. No barriers, no dismissing of crazy stuff – go wild!
Any other options? What if there were no rules?

Capture all your emotions, no matter how crazy they may seem. Then start to filter them to two options and continue in ➡

two parallel streams with the following questions. One of the options should very soon present itself as the best way!

To what extent does this meet all your objectives?
What are your criteria and measurements for success?
What intermediate steps might there be?
When precisely are you going to start and finish each action step?
What could arise to hinder you in taking these steps?
What personal resistance do you have, if any, to taking these steps?
Who needs to know what your plans are?
What support do you need, and from whom?
What will you do to obtain that support, and from whom?
What will you do to obtain that support, and when?

Now you know where you are going, and the reason why, and you have a fair idea of a top-level plan of action, one that you believe will work. You looked at many options and did not rush to select the one that is a best fit with the best chance of success.
So let's get into some detail, and let's also reconfirm your commitment to the move.

Way ahead/will
Which option do you feel strongly about? Why?
What's the first step?
When are you going to start?
What do you need to consider to make it happen?
What resources (time, money, etc.)?
What help?
Who can help you with this? How can you persuade them to help?
What else can you do to help achieve the goal?
How will you ensure you set aside enough time?
What are you going to stop doing to give you the time to do this?
How strong is your belief that you will make it happen? ➡

Really? Anything less than 7 out of 10 and go back to the beginning!

What barriers will get in your way? Greatest challenge?

How can you increase your self-belief?

What support do you need from me (the team leader)?

How will you celebrate success? With whom?

How will you stay in this new place and not slip back to where you were?

Cracking! You've got it! You know what you want and why. You've been made more conscious of where you are now and the benefits of moving on. You looked at all the options, chose one, planned it and are committed to the new you. How exciting is that! Just go and do it. Now! Don't delay!

Notes

_____

_____

_____

_____

_____

_____

_____

_____

_____

_____

_____

EPILOGUE

I sincerely hope that you enjoyed and continue to enjoy my book and use it as a constant reference! I have tried to make it as UMU as possible.

It is the culmination of all my experiences and learning to date and every single aspect of the activities within have been refined over the years and proven to be hugely effective. As you take away the lessons from my book and apply them to all areas of your life, I would like to know what happens. I am, like you, on a continuous journey of discovery and learning and would welcome your feedback, thoughts and personal experiences.

Let us create a community, a ground-swell of Compassionate Leadership that will change the way we work together to ensure that in all walks of life we:

'secure the best for and the best out of all'.

To share your thoughts and experiences about this book, please drop me a line at compassion@manleytalks.com, and if I can help you or your organisation on your journey then please just ask!

When I dedicated the book to 'you' at the beginning, I sincerely meant it. It is my expressed wish and intent that maybe, through my ramblings and learning, your journey could be made sweeter and more meaningful.

Hurrah!

INDEX

NOTES

THE COMPASSIONATE LEADERSHIP ACADEMY

The brand-new online **Compassionate Leadership Academy (CLA)** is a continuation of Manley's work that will transform the way you can access exceptional leadership development.

Designed to further the accessibility and the impact of compassionate leadership worldwide, we want to create a 'compassionate movement' that fundamentally changes the way we engage with the workplace, with each other and our wider communities, spreading compassion across the globe.

- A hugely interactive, online, six-month programme to qualify as a compassionate leader

- Plus a six-month masterclass compassionate leadership programme

- Delivered by Manley in his very personal and personable style

- Accessible on all devices, online and offline, priced and designed to disrupt the market and challenge existing thinking on e-learning

- Based on deep research into the physiology and psychology of learning

- Democratising access to quality leadership development

- Love the learning and 'be the change you want to see in the world'

Enjoy the journey

Register now at www.cla-global.com